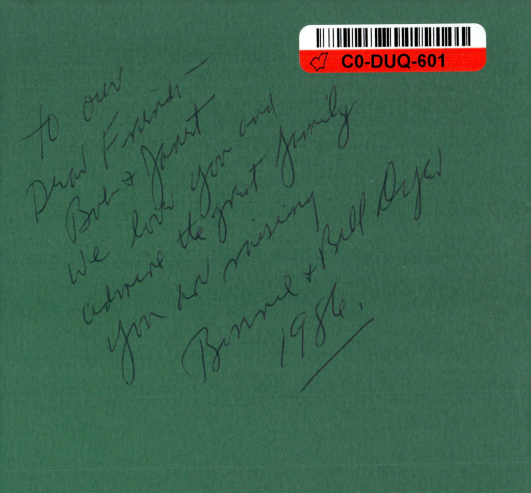

To our
Dear Friends —
Bob & Janet —
We love you and
admire the great family
you are raising
Bonnie & Bill Dyke
1986.

EFFECTIVE MORMON FAMILIES

EFFECTIVE MORMON FAMILIES

HOW THEY SEE THEMSELVES

William G. Dyer and Phillip R. Kunz

Deseret Book Company
Salt Lake City, Utah

No part of this book may be reproduced in any
form or by any means without permission in writing
from the publisher, Deseret Book Company,
P.O. Box 30178, Salt Lake City, Utah 84130.
Deseret Book is a registered trademark of
Deseret Book Company, Inc.

ISBN 0-87579-059-3
Library of Congress Catalog Card Number 86-71891

First printing November 1986

CONTENTS

EFFECTIVE MORMON FAMILY QUIZ

This book represents findings about how 200 Mormon families, rated as highly effective, live, think and act. Here are a set of questions about these families. See how closely you can estimate the results of our survey. Answers follow the quiz.

1. What percent of these families said they always paid tithing?
   A. 99%
   B. 90%
   C. 82%

2. What percent said they always had daily prayer?
   A. 80%
   B. 50%
   C. 29%

3. What percent said they always or usually held a weekly family home evening?
   A. 50%
   B. 66%
   C. 83%

4. What percent said they always accepted Church jobs?
   A. 93%
   B. 70%
   C. 54%

5. What percent said they always or usually read scriptures daily?

   A. 28%

   B. 40%

   C. 55%

6. What percent said the family always or usually did things together?

   A. 50%

   B. 74%

   C. 96%

7. What percent said they always discussed family problems together?

   A. 52%

   B. 70%

   C. 83%

8. What percent said they always did household chores together?

   A. 70%

   B. 51%

   C. 32%

9. What percent said their children's friends had been very helpful in influencing their children for good?

   A. 95%

   B. 85%

   C. 60%

10. Which activity involved the most family members outside the home?

    A. Job

    B. Sports

    C. Dates

11. What did these families say was their top special strength?

    A. They work together
    B. They love each other
    C. They help each other

12. What did these parents say was their most important method of teaching their children?

    A. Provide good books
    B. Have effective family night
    C. Set a good example

13. How strict did these families feel they were compared to other families?

    A. Much stricter
    B. Somewhat stricter
    C. About the same

14. For families that gave an allowance, how much did most give a 14-year-old each week?

    A. Over $10
    B. $5 to $10
    C. $1 to $3

15. What percent said they always or most of the time required children to work for money they get from parents?

    A. 20%
    B. 41%
    C. 55%

16. What percent of the children held a job outside the home while still living at home?

    A. 95%
    B. 80%
    C. 65%

17. How many hours were most 16 to 20-year-olds required to work around the house each week?
    A. None
    B. Five hours or less
    C. More than ten hours

18. What percent of both boys and girls were expected to do the dishes?
    A. 91%
    B. 76%
    C. 52%

19. What percent of older brothers and sisters attended the functions where younger ones performed?
    A. 92%
    B. 82%
    C. 72%

20. What percent of these families kissed each other as a way of showing love to each other?
    A. 85%
    B. 70%
    C. 50%

21. What percent said the first method of showing love to a family was to hug them?
    A. 17%
    B. 30%
    C. 52%

22. What percent of these families said they talked to each child ever day?
    A. 94%
    B. 81%
    C. 64%

23. The biggest number of these families had how many rules in the family?

    A. Less than five
    B . Between five and ten
    C. Over ten

24. Which of these did most families have as a rule?

    A. Help
    B . Be around the house
    C. Tell where you're going

25. What percent of these parents said they always controlled all of the television watching of their children?

    A. 60%
    B . 42%
    C. 24%

26. In these families which would most likely be named as a family hero?

    A. A grandparent
    B . Danny Ainge
    C. Marie Osmond

27. What would these families say about the family library as compared to the libraries of others?

    A. Worse than others
    B . About the same
    C. Better than others

28. How much did these families watch television together as a family?

    A. Almost never
    B . Less than 10 hours a week
    C. Over ten hours a week

29. What was the adversity most often faced by these families?

    A. Death
    B. Health problems
    C. Rebellious child

30. What percent said the mother talked to the children more than the father did?

    A. 55%
    B. 68%
    C. 91%

Answers

1. A	7. A	13. B	19. A	25. C
2. C	8. C	14. C	20. A	26. A
3. B	9. B	15. B	21. A	27. C
4. A	10. A	16. A	22. B	28. B
5. A	11. B	17. B	23. A	29. B
6. C	12. C	18. B	24. C	30. B

Chapter One

WHAT THIS BOOK
IS ABOUT

This book is about good Mormon families—families that work. Not perfect families, mind you—there's no such thing. We surveyed nearly two hundred Latter-day Saint couples and none of them came close to claiming they were perfect. But most of them said something like this: "We've got a good family. We love each other. We're proud of our kids. We don't have a magic formula, but we work hard at being a family, and we pray a lot about being parents."

Almost every popular magazine rack and bookstore is loaded with commentary on American families, but most of it concentrates on what's going wrong—drugs, child abuse, incest, teenage pregnancies, abortion, and suicide. Most reports from sociologists and other scholars of the family look at the same things. But what goes on in families that are trying to be effective and, in the main, are succeeding? What do parents and children do in these families? What factors build cohesion and harmony? What keeps children out of trouble and sends them on to form strong marriages and families of their own?

These were the questions in the back of our minds when we started thinking through a research project to find the answers. We'd both been intrigued by Thomas J. Peters and Robert H. Waterman's *In Search of Excellence: Lessons from America's Best-Run Companies*, a popular analysis of how the managers of outstanding U.S. corporations made them that way (New York: Warner Books/Harper & Row, 1982). The book was a number-one best-seller in the

1

United States, for its principles were applicable to much more than business. The authors identified eight conditions that some twenty successful American companies had in common, from McDonald's to Procter and Gamble. Could we use the same approach with families, we wondered?

We think that effective families of any subculture or religion would have most, if not all, of the same characteristics of good Mormon families; but we wanted to see how Latter-day Saint doctrines and practices get translated into family living. Except in Utah and a few scattered communities in the Rocky Mountain area, Mormons are a minority in America. They live, work, go to school, and participate generally in the activity of the communities in which they live. Some of the differences between Mormon teachings and national practices seem to be the kind of things that could lead to greater internal cohesion *or* to potential conflict.

For instance, good Mormons are expected to abstain from alcohol, drugs, tobacco, tea, and coffee. If the parents follow the Word of Wisdom, and if the children accept it too, smoking, drugs, and drinking would not be problems in the family. But if children choose to disregard it, then the resultant confrontations could be even more stressful than in families where drinking might be a health problem but not also a religious issue.

Mormons have an active social life; but for youngsters, there are rules about not dating until age sixteen, no premarital sex, no marriage until after missions, and then marriage in the temple with its high standards for entrance. Young Mormons, surrounded by social alternatives, sometimes struggle with these expectations.

Being a good Mormon involves other expectations: regular family prayer, blessings on the food at every meal, regular church attendance every Sunday for three hours, weekly family council or family night, monthly fasts and donations, tithing, and working hard at church callings. Church emphasis on family also means that couples usually expect to have large families as well as close, loving, and hardworking families. But is there really a connection between doing all these things and having a good family?

We decided to find out. We wrote to selected stake presidents from a number of states and received responses from Washington, Oregon, California, Idaho, Montana, Utah, Texas, and Wyoming. We explained the project and asked them to identify fifteen families they felt were "the best families in their church jurisdiction." We didn't try to define "best families," since the perception of effectiveness itself was one of the things we wanted to study. Interviews later indicated that almost all of the stake presidents used two criteria: the families were active in church and seemed to be united and supportive of each other. We specified that we wanted only families who had children still at home with at least one child old enough to be married or go on a mission, because we wanted parents who had worked through the strains of the teenage years with at least one of their children.

We did some preliminary interviews and, using that information as a guide, constructed a questionnaire, which we sent to approximately three hundred families. About two hundred usable surveys came back, and we held in-depth interviews by telephone and in person with about twenty-five families. From their answers, slightly edited for consistency of style, we selected the principles for effective families that we discuss chapter by chapter in this book.

Although these families have "effectiveness" in common, they are very different in other ways. Some live on farms. Some come from cities, like Salt Lake City, Houston, and Los Angeles. The husbands ranged in age from thirty-four to seventy-eight (average fifty-two) and wives from thirty-one to sixty-five (average forty-nine). The men had had, on the average, sixteen years of education—meaning through four years of college, but the actual years ranged from high-school drop-outs in the tenth grade to those who had had eight years of college. Wives had usually received less education, ranging from ten to nineteen years with an average of 13.7 years. The husbands were doctors, lawyers, managers, craftsmen, farmers, and blue-collar workers. Although most of the women were homemakers by profession, their careers and jobs also included the professions, managerial, secretarial, and blue-collar positions. The smallest number of children was three, the largest number twenty-one for the men (including second marriages), and fourteen for the women. The average was a little over six children per family. In contrast, nationally the average couple has 2.1 children.

Is this study representative of all Mormon families? Obviously not. This sample of active families doesn't tell us what a good Mormon family in Germany, Japan, or Peru might be like. We *think* they'd be similar, but we don't know. Families where only one parent is a Mormon might also be very effective, but our survey didn't try to find out how. Furthermore, younger parents may have different philosophies of parenting that result in different but equally effective families. But our study was not meant to include them.

We didn't try to get a control group of "ineffective" families, but we asked some bishops and stake presidents, who knew their congregations rather well, for some names of Latter-day Saints that, in their opinion and for whatever reasons, just weren't doing as well with their children, then did some limited surveying and conducted about thirty-five interviews in Utah, Idaho, and Wyoming, trying to identify some of the differences.

Despite the limitations of the sample, we think the study does give a clear picture of what goes on in most Mormon families with parents who have a strong commitment to the Church and who feel that their parenthood is a stewardship from the Lord.

One of the valuable parts of doing this project was the insight it gave both of us into our own families. Both of us had felt that we were the only parents we knew doing certain things; but as the surveys came back, we discovered that many families had independently made the same connections. We both also learned about techniques and activities we wished we'd known about earlier.

Bill: Neither my wife, Bonnie Hansen Dyer, nor I came from a traditional Mormon home. My father, George William Dyer, never joined the church, and my mother, Ada Gibb, was a fiercely devout Mormon, so we seven children were reared in a split family. I never experienced family prayer, going together to church, a father's blessing, or an admininstration. My father was forty-nine when he married, and my mother was thirty-two. Because my father was in his fifties by the time children started coming along, he didn't involve himself much in our activities. Neither of my parents drove, so we didn't go far from home—a little corner grocery store with an attached house on the outskirts of Portland Oregon.

Bonnie's family was also atypical. Her father, Clarence Hansen, died when she was six months old, leaving her mother, Wyroa Hansen, to rear four small children alone, first in Spring City, Utah, but later in Provo, where her mother taught school to support the family.

We met in 1949 at BYU just after I returned from a Southern States Mission. I was twenty-four, and Bonnie was twenty-one. We had both been active in church and had absorbed the lessons from the manual about ideal family life, but we married without a role model about how an active LDS mother and father built a family together. And we both wanted a good family—a loving, caring, sharing family.

Our first child, Gibb (William, Jr.), was born when I just started my first teaching job at Iowa State University. Then Michael, Lisa, Jeff, and David all followed in rather rapid succession, all born in Provo, after I had returned in 1955 to teach at BYU. All along the way, we tried to figure out how to be good parents.

We watched the behavior of families we admired in the branches and wards where we lived, read books on child rearing and family relations, and tried to follow the counsel of Church leaders. This led us to a general pattern of Church-directed activity. We made sure we went to all meetings with out children. We accepted Church assignments and tried to have regular family prayer and family night. But some of the activities in our family just seemed to emerge out of experience. A family pattern—one of the healthiest, in retrospect—was the evening drift into our bedroom, where all the children would end up piled on the bed with us, rehashing the day, shooting the breeze, swapping stories, and communicating a lot of affection. We were the only family we knew that did such a "crazy" thing, but I was pleased from the survey to see that most effective families talk a lot and sometimes develop unusual traditions to be sure there's time to talk. Whatever the elements of the Dyer mix, we've been very satisfied with the results. All of our children have graduated from college, the boys have all gone on missions, and now all four children have been married in the temple.

Now that Bonnie and I have the pleasures and perplexities of grandparenthood to deal with, we can look back on those parenting years with a great deal of gratitude, some satisfaction, and the feeling every parent has of knowing there were just a few things we'd like to change.

Phil: Any sociologist gets used to people asking, "What kind of research are you doing? Oh? Mmmm." But not with this project. Nearly everyone who has learned about it has wanted to know more. Many of the people who participated in the survey went the second mile and sent us letters and lengthy comments on the questionnaire. During the interviews, they wanted to know what other families were doing. I shared their interest. Gathering the data and analyzing it helped me understand more about my family, feel reinforced in the things we were doing right, and feel motivated to change in areas where we need to do better.

Both my wife, Joyce Sheffield Kunz, and I came from

6

what would be considered strong, active families. My mother, Hilda Stoor, was a convert to the Church just before her marriage to my father, Parley P. Kunz, who was already a third-generation member of the Church. My parents were farmers and ranchers in Bern, Idaho. I was born in the house where my father had been born, a house *his* father had built. Our mountain village had been founded by my great-grandfather, John Kunz II, who had been sent to Bear Lake by Brigham Young to develop the cheese industry. Even now, only three of Bern's bishops have not been named Kunz. My father was one of those Kunz bishops.

At the beginning of his ten-year term, he was promised that if he kept the commandments he would live to see all of his thirteen children grow to maturity. As we brothers and sisters gathered once in 1983 and again in 1985 to bury our eighty-nine-year-old father and our eighty-five-year-old mother, we thought of that promise. The youngest child is now over forty years of age.

Our home was a home of twice-daily family prayer, missions, temple-going, tithing, and a lot of work and play within the family. There were spankings, heartaches, and trials, but we also experienced a lot of love. I grew up knowing that my parents supported and loved me. I grew up knowing that they expected me to succeed in something.

Joyce also grew up in a home of Church tradition, as a seventh-generation Church member. Her father, Kenneth H. Sheffield, was a member of the general board of the Young Men's Mutual Improvement Association and had been for some twenty years. He was the coordinator for MIA June Conference for many years up until the time of his death in an automobile accident. Joyce grew up in a home based on family prayer, temple-going, missions, and service to the Church. Her father was involved in Scouting all of his life and with young people, and worked as a seminary teacher, a principal, and an area coordinator. Even into her eighties, her mother, Lucile Beck Sheffield, was a diligent participant in the genealogy extraction program. She, like my mother, labored in the Church all her life.

Thus, the pattern for our own home was one centered within the Church. We both saw a method of producing a family that had worked, and we tried to bring the principles we learned into our own family. After I served in the army in Germany, I filled a mission to the Southern States, where my companions and I had several dozen converts. At Brigham Young University, where I obtained a B.S. and an M.S., I met Joyce and fell in love. Our son Jay was born when I was a senior, putting Joyce's degree on slow-down. We moved to Lyman, Wyoming, where I taught seminary for a year and where Jenifer was born on a minus-37-degree day. Ann Arbor came next with a Ph.D. in sociology, then a year teaching in Laramie, Wyoming. We had waited and hoped for another child for a long time, then when Jody was born, almost simultaneously, Joyce's father was killed at the height of his achievement. We then returned to Provo, where I taught at Brigham Young University, Joyce finished her B.S. in elementary education, and our family was rounded out with Johnathon Kenneth (named for his grandfathers), and Jana. Our eldest son served a mission in Germany, married Rebecca Neumann from Illinois, and is now in graduate school. He was followed into the mission field by Jenifer, who has learned to love the people of Uruguay. Our remaining three children are also looking forward to these kinds of experiences.

In other words, this has not been an abstract project. Even though we've been careful in our research and methodology, it has more than intellectual interest for us. There *are* some principles that underlie the creation of a good family. For both of us, this project has been personally rewarding. Phil and Joyce come from traditional Mormon families. Bill and Bonnie do not. Yet the activities and results in both families have been very similar.

The memorable opening line of Tolstoy's *Anna Karenina* is: "Happy families are all alike; every unhappy family is unhappy in its own way." Happy LDS families are certainly not clones of each other, but it was remarkable to us that there was so much consensus. Here is a profile of an effective family's characteristics, characteristics discussed a chapter at a time in the rest of the book.

1. In an effective LDS family, the parents choose Church activity and gospel values as the foundation of their home. Many of our effective parents had come from strong LDS homes and were continuing a pattern they had grown up in, but a remarkably high number had not. Their independent decision was enough to make the difference for their children. (Chapter 2.)

2. The family is characterized by love and unity. The parents put their children above work, recreation, and friends. Siblings are more important than friends. Family time is more important than time spent on anything else. (Chapter 3.)

3. Discipline grows out of high expectations and clear communication. Parents start with praising and rewarding positive behavior. If there's a problem, talking it out is the first response. In fact, talking seems to be one of the favorite activities of the whole family, any time, any place. (Chapter 4.)

4. Parents consider teaching one of their most important jobs. The Church is important, but they hold themselves responsible for their children's knowledge of the gospel. Furthermore, learning is an important job for the children, a fact that influences the parents' strong support of public education, attitudes toward television, and reading habits. (Chapter 5.)

5. In an effective family, you can see the affection. Hugs, kisses, and verbal "I love you's" are common. (Chapter 6.)

6. Effective families have a variety of styles for teaching the children about the importance of work (starting with household chores) and money (including allowances and special rewards). But all of them do it in some way. (Chapter 7.)

7. After a minimum of twenty years of marriage, the husband-wife relationship is not perfect but it's pretty good—in fact, an average 8.5 on a scale of 10. The couple has learned how to make decisions, deal with the world around them, and handle issues of intimacy. (Chapter 8.)

8. No family is immune from difficulty. Effective families handle floods, wayward children, health problems, aging parents, and money problems with three techniques: they seek the Lord's help, they pull together, and they learn to endure. (Chapter 9.)

9. Children in these families usually get along well with others and have lots of friends, but siblings have more of an impact on them and, next to the president of the Church, a member of the family is most likely to be the family hero. (Chapter 10.)

10. Effective families have goals: the parents know what they want for their children in gospel living, education, economic stability, and relationship skills. And for the family as a whole, the goal is "being together forever." (Chapter 11.)

In chapter 12, we discuss how these effective parents have felt about how well they were doing as parents when their children were at different ages. We also discuss how to initiate change if things aren't going well or could be going better.

Finally, in chapter 13, we take a look at some trends in families, nationwide and in the Church. What does the pattern look like for the future? Can this pattern of success be replicated in another generation? Will other techniques need to be developed?

For us and our wives, family living is a great adventure—strenuous, taxing, and immensely rewarding. The insight into the process of family living shared by the couples we've met in doing this research has been our great pleasure.

Chapter Two

"WE CHOSE THE
CHURCH":
THE PARENTS'
FOUNDATION
VALUES

Although successful families are far from being identical, nearly all of them share the characteristics outlined in chapter 1. Of those characteristics, the single most important—unvarying, unanimous, and preeminent—is that the parents have made a public and private commitment to the Church and gospel principles. This commitment is the foundation value of their homes.

The last question in our survey asked: "Looking over all of the kinds of issues we have raised and any others you may think of, what do you consider has been most important to make you a strong LDS family?"

Typical answers were: "We feel we truly love the Lord" and "Trying to live the principles of the gospel." "Consistent activity in the Church," said a Montana family with six children by the husband's first marriage and two by the second. One couple wrote: "The thing that has been most important to us in our family is the great feelings we have about the gospel. We know what the purpose of life is and we know why our children are important. Our whole life revolves around the Church. Heavenly Father is a partner for us, and we certainly count on him to assist us after we have done our part. We can forego a lot of things that neighbors have because we know that helping a child to be successful will pay more in the end than a bigger house or a boat. Missions, temple marriage, and sticking close together—*that's* what's important to us."

When we asked parents to identify the most important

positive factor in making them a strong LDS family, 96 percent gave one of two answers (or both): forty-two percent
mentioned the Church and its programs; 54 percent cited
personal religious practices such as prayer, or their feelings
of faith. Early in the questionnaire, we asked several questions about typical Mormon activities that probably most
people would take for granted in active families and asked
parents to say whether they always, usually, sometimes, or
seldom did them. The activities were:

1. We attend Church.
2. We pay tithing.
3. We have family prayer morning and night.
4. We have weekly family home evening.
5. We attend the temple regularly.
6. We read the scriptures regularly as a family.
7. We accept Church jobs.

The most important activities were attendance at Church
meetings, paying tithing, and accepting Church jobs.
Ninety-nine percent of the couples said they *always* paid
their tithing. Ninety-seven percent indicated they *always*
attended Church, and 93 percent responded that they *always* accepted Church callings or assignments.

We also gave these parents a list of six goals that
seemed fairly typical of LDS families and asked them to
check the items that were "special goals" for them. The
goals were:

1. Have children get a good education   99 percent
2. Have children marry in the temple   99 percent
3. Help each child develop a strong
   feeling of self-worth or good self-concept 99 percent
4. Develop a strong sense of family unity   98 percent
5. Have everyone active in the Church   97 percent
6. Have children go on a mission   94 percent

Note that the first three percentages are tied, but the first
three goals do not, in our opinion, represent a mixture of

secular and religious goals. The Church's emphasis on education and self-esteem both have theological bases summarized in the common phrases "I am a child of God" and "the glory of God is intelligence."

Parents talked about how closely these goals were connected. "If we could help each child develop a good self-concept, then reaching all the other goals would be simpler," said the parents of five. A father of six noted: "If one of the kids feels dumb or untalented and ends up not doing well in school, even for a short time, we really worry about that and take steps to see that he or she gets some successful experiences. I've seen too many youngsters who feel stupid in school start hanging out with friends who aren't doing well, get involved in drugs, marry inappropriately and too soon, and spend the rest of their lives struggling, never making a good living, never feeling good about themselves, and usually getting a divorce. When kids are doing well in school and are really involved in what's going on in church, it just seems to close the door on a whole bunch of negative possibilities." In their own ways, many other parents expressed their own feelings about the interconnectedness of self-esteem, economic security, and Church service.

We also asked parents to identify other goals that they had for their families. (See chapter 11.) Answers included "Be happy." "Be together in the celestial kingdom." "Teach each child to function as a mature, responsible, independent person as early as possible." "Have fun as a family." The families in this study also placed a high priority on teaching their children good work habits. "Teach them the importance of working and taking pride in what they do," said the parents of nine who run a farm. Other parents said similar things: "Be self-reliant and dependable." "Teach them to work, save money, and be honest."

And lest all of this sound desperately determined, many families listed "having fun together" and "having a good sense of humor" as part of their family pleasures and goals. Mormons have long been known for their industriousness and integrity. It is no accident that these highly effective parents articulate the same values for themselves and their children.

"WE DECIDED . . . "

We asked a cluster of questions trying to find out where this commitment to the Church came from and were impressed to discover, once again, the principle of agency. Commitment did not just happen, and it wasn't just programmed into parents by their own parents. It was a conscious decision, and we were encouraged to discover that it could take place at almost any point in the marriage. In other words, you don't have to come from a strong LDS family yourself to have one. Forty-nine percent of the husbands and 39 percent of the wives had not graduated from seminary. Only 21 percent of the husbands had been on missions. Twenty percent of the fathers and 18 percent of the mothers were not baptized at age eight. Between 15 and 18 percent were baptized after the age of twelve.

Of course, many parents came from active homes, some from homes where they were fourth-, fifth-, and sixth-generation Mormons. But at some point, sometimes before marriage, sometimes as a couple, these people decided that their own children would be raised in a gospel environment. For some, the point of decision was very clear. For others, the decision was so logical that there didn't seem to be an alternative. However, they followed it up with action. It's the action that seems to separate highly effective couples from less effective couples. One Utah couple with seven children described the process succinctly: "We simply made up our minds, as parents, that we were going to be a strong LDS family and put all our time and energies into accomplishing it. The father had many, many Church callings. The mother and children joyfully supported him in them. We have tried to teach the children to be aware of the blessings that have come to us as a family for doing so."

For a more extended example, let's look at a couple

we'll call Harvey and Joan, who live in the Bay Area. They chose a different pattern than the one they saw in their own homes when they began rearing their children. Early in their marriage, they made conscious decisions to be active in the Church. Joan's father was not only inactive but hostile to the Church, though her mother felt more supportive and encouraged Joan to participate, especially while she was a teenager. A brother was killed during World War II when Joan was fourteen, and she began seeking religious understanding from that point. When she went to college at Berkeley, she began attending LDS institute of religion classes, where she met and began dating Harvey.

Harvey came from a split family. His father was not a Mormon and his mother was not active. However, she had had Harvey blessed as a baby and baptized at age eight. He became a fairly active member on his own. Harvey and Joan dated, fell in love, and married while they were still in college. Harvey graduated, but Joan stopped when the first of their seven children was born.

Although neither of them had learned religious activity from their parents, they knew they wanted their own family to be different, and the model of the large, loving family engrossed in Church service appealed to them. They admired the active Mormon families they saw in the ward, particularly how close and happy they seemed. "Love, respect, and being happy together, that's what we wanted," they said. "We knew we wanted a different family life than the kind we came from." They decided to adopt the activities that the Church recommended as ways of reaching that goal: daily prayer, weekly family night, regular church attendance, and obedience to Church standards. Harvey blessed the children as babies, baptized them at age eight, and usually ordained his sons to the priesthood.

Harvey also regularly gave the children priesthood blessings—administering to them when they were ill and giving them special father's blessings on important events like birthdays, the first day of school, going away from home, leaving for a mission or marriage, and so on. "In ad-

15

dition to the very real blessings that he called down on them," Joan said, "I realize now that it was a way of telling each child, 'You're important to us. We know that starting school is important to you. We're all in this together, and we want you to be successful.'"

Harvey and Joan were talented, committed, and creative. From the earliest days of their marriage, each always had a demanding Church assignment. Harvey even served as a bishop. Joan wonders, "As I look back on those early years with several young children, maybe we were too busy, but we seemed to survive successfully. We always felt that we belonged to a group of people who cared about us and our children, no matter what ward we lived in. We felt that our children grew up feeling accepted at church, happy to be there, and happy to help."

Perhaps most important, Joan says, "We tried to live consistently. If we told the children we believed something, we didn't feel we had the right to show something different in our actions. We never asked the children to do things that we didn't do ourselves. We hope that this attitude can carry on in the families of our children and grandchildren."

Interestingly enough, one mother of seven sees the children as having a great influence on their decision to be active in the Church. Like Harvey and Joan, she and her husband had both been raised by inactive Mormon parents. They were hard-working, he as county road superintendent and she as school cook after the children were older. As a couple, they wanted more and decided, after the birth of their fifth child, to go to the temple. "We wanted what the Church had to provide for our children," she recalls, "but we counted on the teachers to give our children the desire to pray and to do what Heavenly Father wanted them to."

They had two more children and, as the children grew older, the parents made an important discovery. They wrote: "We had been blessed with seven fine spirits who wanted something in their home that we hadn't necessarily thought about having earlier. We could have filled out the whole questionnaire with different answers, depending on which point in our marriage we referred to."

MIXED FEELINGS

Ironically, we found that many couples in the survey whose family values are inseparably entwined with gospel values still feel somewhat apologetic or guilty because, although they are carrying out a Church program, they are not doing it the "Church way" and feel that their families would work even better if somehow they could do it "by the book." They genuinely want to do everything the Church teaches them to do, and they want to do it perfectly. Yet in these effective families, they do not feel paralyzed by the desire for perfection. The statistics and interviews paint a remarkable picture of being simultaneously contented with family strengths while never feeling they can say "We've got it made." These mixed feelings should, however, be read in the light of a historical gap; many of the programs now being advocated for families have come along in the last few years when family patterns were already set. Each of the families in this survey had at least one child old enough for marriage or missions and averaged six children. In other words, the parents are reporting on a busy household where at least some children are working full time or part time, going to school, living away from home at school, or married.

At some point, it will be interesting to see if families with younger children—those who have grown up with this new battery of Church programs for families—have established and maintained a different pattern for five "test" activities: temple attendance, family prayer, family night, scripture study, and keeping personal journals.

Temple Attendance

Despite the importance of the temple in Mormon theology and beliefs, only 24 percent of these couples indicated that they "always" go to the temple regularly. An additional one-third attended the temple "seldom" or "sometimes." However, many of the couples explained their answers, anxious not to have their feelings about the temple misunderstood. It was easy to understand the couple from Texas before the construction of the Dallas Temple. They wrote: "We live several hundred miles from the nearest temple. As a result we only go to the temple on certain special occasions. We probably could go more, but it is a major effort."

Other couples had the same situation. One Montana couple said, "We always go when we're traveling near a temple." Another family plans summer vacations to include a day at the temple but lives twelve hundred miles away from the nearest one. Another couple two hundred miles away from the nearest temple attends "approximately three times a year."

Even where distance from a temple is not great, other priorities may come first. One Utah couple confessed, "Our schedules are so tight that we often have to cancel plans to attend the temple. We feel bad when this happens, and the children know we're disappointed." One father discussed the idea of "seasons" in relation to temple attendance: "We don't go to the temple as often as we would like to, but there are a lot of things going on. When we were in graduate school we had to study and since that time we have been trying to verify our four generation sheets in the genealogy program. In our family we think the scripture about the season for all things is correct. The season for more temple attendance is not right now. Oh, we go as often as we can—about once or twice a month. We try to go when a relative is married or on other special occasions. My grandparents just about lived in the temple the last twenty years of their lives, which was great for them, but they didn't do that when they were trying to make a living on the farm and raising their children. We look forward to the time when we can go more than we do."

Our view is that attendance once or twice a month demonstrates a substantial commitment, but it does help explain why this family—and probably others—foresee a more intensive season of temple activity after the children are gone. Temple attendance does not involve the whole family. Usually the parents go together, leaving the children at home, although occasionally the returned missionary son or daughter or married children who live nearby might join the parents as a special occasion. Still, the temple itself represents an unquestionably high value in effective Mormon families. Almost all of effective couples were either married or sealed in the temple (in a couple of cases, distance had been prohibitive); all of them want their children to marry in the temple. All show strong support for temple attendance, even though their regular attendance is not as high as one might assume that it would be.

Family Prayer

In addition to temple attendance, other religious activities that are stressed in lessons but that don't show up as top priorities for these effective families include regular family prayer, regular family home evenings, and regular scripture study as a family. And nearly all of the families described the guilty gap between an ideal they accept and the tough realities of getting through a day.

Twenty-eight percent of the families said they "always" held morning and evening family prayer, and 45 percent said they "usually" did—making a total of 73 percent that usually had prayer together. A common comment was, "We almost always get the family together for prayer once during the day but not every morning and evening."

Also, part of the problem may be in the families' definitions of family prayer. In an interview, one father said with some feelings of frustration and resignation, "Given the ages and situations of our children, it is almost impossible to have regular family prayer. Some work right after school until rather late. They aren't here for evening prayer and don't want to get up when others have to be up and gone for early morning seminary. Then when you add in different ones having practices, games, meetings—it just seems the family is not all together to have regular prayer. What we do is to have a prayer when we bless the food with all those who are here, and I know that all of us say our private prayers. But regular morning and evening prayer with all of the family just seems to be practically impossible."

Another family that clearly seemed to hold what we would call "family prayer" didn't think they were: "We have family prayer once in a while, but it is hard to do since our children work out of the home. We are seldom all home at the same time. We pray with whoever is there—sometimes only four or five us at a time, but that is all we can get together. Sometimes there may just be the two of us or only one of the children with us. On Sunday we can usually all pray together in family prayer."

Family Home Evening

Only 18 percent of the families said they "always" held a family home evening each week. An additional 48 percent "usually" held family home evening, bringing the total to 66 percent. The remaining one-third said they held it "sometimes" or "seldom."

Family home evening was instituted as a formal program only in the early 1960s; many of the families in our sample had already established other patterns with the children that did not involve a pre-formatted "meeting", so many of them probably said they were not holding family home evening. "Our last girl is leaving for college," wrote one Idaho mother of seven. "When there were other children at home, we had family home evening and family prayer regularly." But with almost all the children gone and the husband working night shift, these programs no longer seemed to fit the family's needs. Several other families said that the program worked better with younger children than with older ones.

Still, many families spent time together regularly and accomplished many of the goals of the program. For example, a regular Sunday dinner-table topic would be about the lessons presented in Sunday School and Primary that day. One mother wrote, "We spend more time together as a family than most other families we know. We read together regularly—scriptures and other books. We play games together, work together, and eat together." Many families hold extended discussions about the scriptures, problems of life, personal and family problems, and plans for a particular project. One of these families, which seems to be characterized by an extraordinarily high level of family interaction, still said somewhat apologetically: "We can see the value of the family home evening lessons to us. It is too bad that we didn't get those lesson manuals earlier in our married life. I guess we did do a lot of that sort of thing but not as well as the book does now."

Family Scripture Study

Only 28 percent of the families in this study indicated that they regularly read the scriptures together. Considerably more hold family home evening than read the scriptures. Sixty-six percent or two-thirds of the families said they "usually" or "always" held family home evening, and one-third said this activity was carried out only "sometimes" or "seldom." Scripture reading was markedly less. Over 70 percent of the families said that scripture reading as a family was done only "sometimes" or "seldom."

When it works, it seems to be rewarding. One Utah father described in an interview how they were doing on the project: "Our stake president used to talk in stake conference about how each morning they were reading the scriptures as a family. We felt that we should do it too, but it's tough to find time for it. We talked with the children who are still living at home, and they wanted to do it. We finally decided that we could read for a while if everyone got up ten minutes earlier. We read about four or five days a week now. So far we have read the Book of Mormon, the Doctrine and Covenants, and the Pearl of Great Price, and now we are in the New Testament. We start reading around the breakfast table while my wife is putting the final touches on breakfast, and that seems to work well."

In one family where the father is disabled and the family has been under considerable financial pressure, the mother wrote that one of their greatest strengths as a family came from "our family mornings where we sing, read the scriptures, and pray together every day."

One Utah mother of six, ages twenty-two to six, who filled out the questionnaire alone, noted that the family studied the scriptures regularly and, in fact, that their three most important rules were: "Everyone comes to scripture study, everyone goes to church, and everyone comes to family home evening." An explanatory note clarified: "Mom sets up these rules, gets everyone up, and prepares the lesson, and Dad comes if he feels like it."

Several families said that individual study works well for them. One Wyoming father listens to tapes of the scriptures while he's working and the children play them at bedtime. Another mother includes taped stories from the scriptures as part of the family activities. One California family of four reads individually, following the schedule in the priesthood manual, and then discusses their readings together. Still other families try to make scripture reading an important part of their family home evenings.

Personal Journals

Another area of Church-family activity particularly stressed by President Spencer W. Kimball during his presidency was keeping a journal. Twenty-five percent of the fathers indicated they write in a journal regularly, and 45 percent of the mothers said they make regular journal entries. The children's activities in this area are almost the same as mother's—about 48 percent. These results suggest that children reared with journal writing as a Church program may adopt the practice at a higher level than their parents.

LESS-EFFECTIVE FAMILIES

Even though parents felt that they could be doing better at Church-related family goals and worked hard to see that they and their children were involved in Church activity, there was no sense that they had turned part of child rearing over to the Church. Many expressed gratitude for help from the Sunday School, a Scout leader, or an outstanding Young Women leader; but they saw it as supplemental. As one mother said, "We are happy for the programs of the Church. Programs seem to come up to help various children from time to time. Nevertheless, we realize the whole thing is ours. If we fail in our home, we are responsible. If a child goes astray, we can't say that he had a bad Sunday School teacher, can we? That wouldn't buy much sympathy."

Among the less-effective LDS families that we interviewed, we were intrigued to find that at least one family still functioned very well as a family though without much Church activity. Beth had come from a long line of Mormon pioneers and was proud of it, even though her family did not attend church regularly and did not hold regular family prayer. She met Jim, a non-Mormon, at BYU, and they married. They went to church occasionally, their six children were blessed and baptized, and Jim was also baptized. Moral behavior and educational achievement were strong family values, and the children have grown up to be close to each other and mutually supportive. Most consider themselves to be Mormon but are not deeply committed to LDS practices.

Most of the less-effective families that we interviewed, however, had not been able to maintain very close ties to the Church. One Wyoming father of five had started smoking, then no longer felt comfortable at church. "Things have been pretty much downhill since then," he said. Another couple who had not been worthy to qualify for a temple marriage admitted, "Then it just got to be easy to stay away from Church." A third couple "just never did get around to" holding family home evening and family prayer although they said they "probably should have." Another Utah mother with three teenagers felt that it was too late to start holding family prayer: "My kids would probably just laugh at the idea."

Couples in our highly effective group, however, are clear about the role of the gospel and the Church in their families' successes. One Salt Lake City professional couple with six children wrote: "Without question, the gospel has been the most important factor in making us a strong family. We don't know how families function in this world without this knowledge and without the influence of the Spirit. We're not just saying this because it sounds good or is expected of us. It is *true* for our family."

In short, the couples who have made a decision that they want a thoroughly Mormon family have found that personal values and institutional values work together. Their children receive clear messages that affirm their worth, set high expectations for them, and pay off in feelings of being loved and respected. It's a potent combination.

Chapter Three

"UNITED WE STAND": BUILDING A STRONG FAMILY IDENTITY

When effective families try to put their finger on what makes them successful, an overwhelming majority mention the same two factors: (1) their commitment to Church principles and programs, and (2) a mutual sense of internal bonding, a deep sense of love, caring, and unity. Although we've discussed these factors in two separate chapters, again and again parents in our survey linked them. "The Church and love for each other and the children" were the most important values to an Idaho couple. "We have a testimony of the gospel of Jesus Christ," said a couple from a small Utah town. "We *know* why we are here, and the family is the center of that reason." "We love our children and place the success of the family above material success, professional success, social status, or political recognition," said the Provo parents of seven children ranging in age from twelve to thirty-two. Another Utah couple with seven children said that one factor in their success was "spending lots of one-on-one time, letting our children know they are more important than work, friends, or hobbies."

Without actually using the word very often, *unity* was a concept that these parents described in detail with statements like these: "We work together." "We're on each other's side." "We help each other." "We're each other's best friends."

A Montana couple, parents of ten, said simply, "Each person has a responsibility to the rest of the family." A mother in Washington with five children wrote, "Being in this family means knowing that when everything else in the world is against us, we can come home and feel loved and know that other family members will show that they think we're special." The Idaho parents of eight asserted, "We're all proud to be members of our family." One Utah couple, the parents of ten, even expressed a kind of wistfulness in answering a question about the age at which they found their children easiest to rear. They responded, "Between birth and twelve," explaining, "We were a complete community within our family." An Idaho couple observed, in a backhanded critique of society, "We have been so contented as a family that our children are probably not as outgoing and aggressive as the business world sometimes demands." A mother said, speaking of a strong extended family with actively involved grandparents, aunts, and uncles, "It means something to belong to this family, and our kids know it. Not that we're anything special—well, yes, special—but not exactly."

In our egalitarian society, these parents seemed to be struggling to find the word that earlier generations and other societies would have understood more easily: clans. Without any necessary suspicion of outsiders or any smug superiority, they still sense deeply that being a member of the family—*this* family—makes a big difference. All people aren't equally important. The family comes first, and *then* comes everybody else. That's probably why so many parents, trying to talk about the sense of unity in their family, resorted in frustration to repeating, "We're a *family*."

In less-effective families, this sense of identity and unity may not develop. One mother of three, whose teenagers had been characterized by rebellion, drug abuse, and confrontation, said bleakly, "We're *not* a special family." What makes the difference?

Family identity may take the form of cute T-shirts at family reunions or a joint family savings account, but those are just manifestations that come from a deeper source. Parents communicate to children that they have entered a distinctive society by entering the Walker or the

Thompson family. There's a boundary. They're just different. "Friends are wonderful and great," as one Texas couple, the parents of six, put it, "but families are *eternal.*" "The children would rather do things with family than with peers most of the time," observed the Idaho parents of seven.

As a result of communicating a sense of family specialness, parents find it easy to say, "In *our* family, we do . . . "(or "don't do . . ."), and the children accept it because they understand, even on a level they can't articulate, that belonging to their family means something extra.

One couple phrased the meaning of family this way for their children: "Families are more important than friends. This means we will treat family members better than we treat our friends. And family activities will take precedence over activities with friends."

Sociology is full of examples of families that are highly united around rather antisocial purposes: organized crime, for instance, or just endless bickering. In other words, you can be united without being loving. But love is an element that nearly all of these families linked with their unity when we talked to them.

Do love and unity occur spontaneously, or can you create them as a result of certain kinds of activities? The answer seems to be yes to both questions. Feelings of love generate sharing and caring activities. The success of these activities in turn confirm and strengthen sharing and caring feelings.

VALUING CHILDREN

A clear underlying condition of family unity is the high value that parents place on their children. By society's standards, they have a lot of children—an average of six per family. The average American family has 2.81 members, including the parents or parent. Usually, traditional societies tend to value children somewhat as possessions. The parents of large families have status because children represent sizable financial leverage for the future. Our highly in-

27

dividualistic society tends to see children as unique little planets, orbiting for a time around the parents' sun but soon shooting off into their own space.

These views represent two extremes, but in effective families, the value of children seems to come somewhere in between. The children are definitely individuals but they complete, enrich, and complement an already existing pattern. In other words, children are seen as both giving something and getting something—that sense of family.

"We put our family life above everything else," says one couple. "We always have in mind that we are going to make it work." "Our kids come first," says another couple, "and they know it." A Texas couple with four children from ages twenty-four to sixteen, wrote, "We *really* love and support each other. Our family comes *first.*" Another couple says, "Unconditional love for each other has got to be one of the factors that makes our family work." In contrast, the mother in one of the less-effective families said resignedly, "My husband has never taken any interest in the children. His activities are always more important than mine or theirs. He's never helped me with anything."

In successful families, nearly every couple expressed how eagerly they anticipated the births of their children and how excited the older children were when the younger children arrived. Naturally, the parents had a great deal to do with shaping those feelings. One couple described how they did it: "Before each of the later children came, we would talk with the older ones about the new brother or sister who would come. When the baby began to move in the womb, all of the children would like to feel the movement. It was exciting to them. There were never any phony stories about the stork delivering babies. They all knew that the baby was in mother's tummy and that she would have to go to the hospital so the doctor could help the baby come out. When they asked, 'How did the baby get into Mother's tummy?' we easily explained that Mother and Daddy together started the baby there. Something like planting a seed together so it would grow into a beautiful baby. They also knew that when the new baby came that they would have to help around the house while Mother was in the hospital, and they were all excited when they were told they would get to help tend the new baby."

As a second characteristic, some activities were simply—no questions asked—family activities. In other words, the parents gave clear messages about the priority of family time. Children did not "own" all of their own hours. For example, many parents stressed that attending church was a family activity, a value they enforced and reinforced even when one parent had to go early or stay late to meetings, even when teenagers exasperated them by dawdling during preparation. They did not leave children home and they did not leave children to come on their own. As a result, they communicated two things: the value of church attendance and the value of family participation. Even when the children, at worst, were giving the most grudging of physical compliance, they still learned these two values. Most of the time, of course, they were also hearing in talks and classes a repetition and reinforcement of the same values and goals their parents had taught them at home.

One Idaho family had a delightful variation on this "always in church" rule. When their three eldest surviving children, spaced two years apart, decided to test the rule, the parents countered ingeniously: "We explained to them that they have their free agency about attending Church meetings. If they choose not to honor the Sabbath by attending their meetings and consider it just another day, then they are free to stay home—and do a weekday chore that we assign. So far they have chosen to attend their meetings." A Salt Lake City family of eight, ages twenty-seven to nine, discussed how church attendance never became a problem: "The father has always just led by example and the children follow. The mother also is dedicated and without fanfare. Going to meetings is *just what our family does.* All of our children have chosen sometimes to stay home from church but quickly recognize themselves that they'd rather go." In a whimsical afterthought, the mother added, "We let them choose; and fortunately, they have always chosen well. I don't know what we'd do if they didn't."

SUPPORTING EACH OTHER

Whenever a child or a parent took part in community life outside the family circle, it was still considered a family affair. Everyone went. Everyone was pleased about a family member giving a talk in church or being in a play or program. As children got older and participated in sports or dance or music, everyone would go to the games or recitals. One Utah couple with five children noted: "We attend all of the children's activities: dance, piano recitals, tennis matches, gymnastic meets. We have gone to horseback competitions together for twelve years."

When the parents cannot attend a child's event, they find other ways to communicate their support. One mother indicated how she handled the sheer logistics problem of not being able to be in two places at the same time: "We have a large family, and time does not permit us to go to everything we would like to. If we cannot attend a game in which our son is playing or a meeting where our daughter is speaking, we try to go out of our way to say something about it. For example, a comment like, Brother Briggs told me that you really gave a good talk, helps the child know that we are interested and would have been there if we could have."

Children in such families learned that the achievement of one family member reflected positively on all of them. There was no sense of competition but rather a sense of reinforcement—at least in theory. Most families agreed that they worked toward this feeling but had better success at some times than at others.

FAMILY COURTESY

Most effective parents also established and enforced standards of family courtesy. They did not expect automatic love from their children; they expected to teach it to them. One Utah family with seven children repeated 1 John 4:7 before every meal: "Let us love one another." At times, the tone of voice hardly matched the words, but the sheer repetition, three times a day, week after week, month after month, year after year, gradually sank in.

"We try to give a lot of emotional support to each child," said one set of parents. Another couple said, "We often tell each other we have the best family in the world. There are a lot of hugs and 'I love you's.'" One Utah family has a code word: "Remember . . . ," which means, "Remember I love you." Another family's rule about the same kind of behavior is "Be congenial. There is no excuse for bad manners."

Most parents feel that they should set the example in apologizing when necessary. "We think it is important that our children learn from their mistakes," said one couple. "Therefore we feel we must let them know we make mistakes too; and when we err, we try to admit it."

An Idaho couple explicitly taught their ten children to say "thank you," "please," "I'm sorry," and "I love you." The mother explained, "My husband and I speak to each other that way. It's a thrill to overhear them playing or working and saying, 'Please.' Even salespeople who regularly call on us have commented on the special feeling we have in our home."

Hardly any family would think of quarreling as positive. Most families have rules against it. But a certain amount of quarreling among children sometimes seems inevitable, no matter how strenuously it's discouraged. How do these effective families deal with sibling squabbles?

Many of them have explicit rules about what is and is not acceptable behavior: no fighting, quarreling, or bickering. Parents intervene quickly when they hear voices begin to rise, sometimes to suppress the symptoms by a firm reminder of the rule, sometimes to send the combatants to different rooms, sometimes to talk through the differences and negotiate a compromise, and sometimes to say, "You

31

can settle this disagreement by yourselves in a friendly way with no yelling. Come tell me when you've worked things out." One practical mother of seven always considers fatigue and hunger as possible causes of quarreling. Even if the disagreement is rooted in other causes, the offer of a snack or rest is sometimes enough distraction to derail an explosion.

One mother emphasized a principle that probably most of the families would agree with: "We spend a *lot* of time training our children when they're young. And we don't fight ourselves." Another mother observed that they consciously began praising positive interaction among the children when they noticed that "some of the other family members (our brothers and sisters) spend a good deal of time talking about how much their children fight. I don't think they fight any more than most families, but they keep focusing on it rather than on the good things that happen."

Several of the families reported, with real appreciation, the quality of love among their children. A delightful example came from one Utah family with nine: "The children not only love each other but they respect and enjoy each other. They enjoy talking for hours with each other. Older children work and play with the younger ones. Our seventeen-year-old son took the four-year-old twins along on one of his dates. He thought it was great, but his girlfriend may have been surprised." Another eighteen-year-old boy, one of ten children, spent his summer vacation with his married sister in Connecticut, tending her four children.

TAKING CHARGE OF FAMILY TIME

Another common element in most of these effective families was a deliberate structuring of family time. In one family it was a rule: "Every family member is expected to eat and pray together at least two times daily."

One Utah couple with seven children deliberately plan their time around togetherness. In addition to showing up en masse for recitals, talks, games, baptisms, and ordinations, they "work in the yard together, pulling weeds in the garden in twos and threes or sevens. Mowing the lawn usually sees two working together—and talking. Canning fruit or drying apricots is a family project. Some do all of some jars, which they then enter in the county fair. Every member of the family has won ribbons and trophies which are displayed around the house."

This family also noted: "Although many of our projects are family projects, we also encourage all our children to achieve in some area. We try to plan activities and events that will focus attention for their successes just on them, so they can know the feeling of having family and friends know they have done well. Sometimes helping our boys earn their Eagle Scout rank has taken lots of parental effort. A good report card may require evening study time with the parent learning new things, helping, encouraging, and sometimes insisting. Although our family consumes a lot of popcorn together, it's hardly ever at the movies or in front of the television.

"We try to keep coordinated with a family calendar, filled in at family home evening for as far ahead as possible and quickly reviewed at the breakfast table for the day— after scripture reading but before toast. And occasionally we send out an emergency SOS to our home teacher to please pick up someone from somewhere because something unexpected came up."

One Texas family felt apologetic about not having family home evening every week and family scripture study every day but felt that "spending *good* time together" was one of their strengths as a family. In spite of busy work schedules, they made time to have family parties at home where everyone could invite guests, went to the beach together, went crabbing together, and also went out to dinner together. A Utah family with seven children speculated, "Maybe we should be more 'others' oriented" but listed as traits that make their family special: "We like each other. We're friends as well as family. We enjoy each other's company, are interested in each other and our accomplishments, have a strong sense of loyalty, take pride in one another's achievements, and have fun to-gether." One of the most important activities they do to-gether is "just visiting together—having a lot of laughs."

It was quite common in effective families for family va-cations to be given great importance. During these vaca-tions, the normal routines are suspended and the parents and children can concentrate on enjoying each other in a pleasant setting. In fact, for many families, the time of highest family interaction is the vacation. A significant number of families owned or rented motor homes or camp-ers to make traveling with a large group more convenient. One family has a fifteen-year tradition of "living in swim-ming suits for two weeks" at a beach house in California that they rent from a family they know. The father gets only two weeks vacation in the summer but has willingly chosen to spend it in this way during the major part of his married life: "It has become a family tradition, and everyone loves to go and to be together. . . . We surf, swim, play ball, sunbathe, go out and play tennis or golf nearby, read, play games, eat, and just have a good time. Sometimes other relatives will stop by for a visit and every-one enjoys that. It seems that everyone gets along better on vacation that at any other time during the year. We always take along some old familiar games (Old Maid, Detective, Monopoly) and some new ones like Trivial Pursuit. All our children who have married still want to come back for the family vacation."

A Utah father with five children said: "Early on, we dis-covered that one of the most unifying experiences for our family was to travel or take a family vacation. Since there were no others around to play with, the children had to re-late to each other and to us, and we found that we really en-joyed each other and had fun together. These outings gave us memories that we will share and talk about all our lives. My wife and I adopted a slogan: 'Experiences are more im-portant than things.' Often we were faced with a decision: should we take a family trip or buy a new refrigerator or carpet? Almost always, the trip won out."

TALKING

National studies on family interaction have become popular since about the mid-1960s, when the "generation gap" was discovered. Families, like other social organizations, are beginning to deal with "wellness," making plans and choices to maximize the potential of each family member. While this is becoming a more widespread goal of many families, it is also being translated into programs and plans to help increase the chance of obtaining this wellness. Open communications is one of the most important factors identified in family health so far.

The 200 families in our study would probably concur about the importance of communication—and their family patterns bear out the value. Parents and children in these families talk a lot, willingly spending the time to be with each other. One father put it this way: "I would say if there is one thing that has made a difference in our family, it has been that we have always talked together. When our children were little, they would all climb in our bed and we would talk. The kids loved to hear how we met and got married and all the events around their births and how special each one was. This pattern has continued through high school and college and even now that some are married. It is common to have these older children sit around the bed on the floor and talk until we have to kick them out so we can get some sleep."

Ninety-nine percent of the parents listed "talking" as their most crucial teaching method. Only "example" (100 percent) ranked higher. And when discipline was needed, "talking with" a child was seen as the most important method in 97 percent of the families.

When children do something of merit, 88 percent of the parents respond most frequently with verbal praise. In fact, almost any change in children's behavior in these families—good or bad—produces increased communication.

Effective fathers and mothers perceive themselves as spending a remarkably high amount of time talking with each child each day. We asked parents how often they engaged in the following activities:

1. Sit around talking together
   as a family   daily 68%   weekly 25%
2. Talk to each child   daily 81%   weekly 12%
3. Talk with children about
   their personal concerns   daily 42%   weekly 41%

Parents also said that the father and mother spent on the average twenty-five minutes a day together talking with *each* child. Additionally mothers claimed they averaged thirty-three minutes daily taking with each child while fathers averaged about eighteen minutes. In families with six children, this could amount to three hours a day for husband and wife together, an extremely high figure, especially when the husband would reportedly spend another two hours in private conversation with the children and the wife another three hours. If they are accurate in this perception, talking together has an extremely high priority. Almost certainly some parents included time spent talking as a group, for some of them specified mealtimes and dinner times as conversational hours when more than one child would be present. It would be interesting to follow this up with more study that would include the parents' perception of time spent in group conversation with two or more children and children's perceptions of the time their parents spent in both private and group conversation with them.

We asked parents, "Overall, who talks to the children most?" Sixty-eight percent said that the mother talked with the children most. Out of all the families only two (1 percent) said the father talked to the children most. Another 27 percent said that both parents talked to the children equally but at separate times.

One mother felt that the figures might not represent family interactions accurately and added, "I know I spend more time talking with the children than my husband does.

But the children respect their father very much and look up to him as the spiritual head of our home. When he does talk to the children either alone or all together, they usually listen very carefully." Another mother also agreed that she spent more time talking to the children than her husband did, but when she baldly asked them, "Who's the boss?" they "all agreed Dad was. I am probably more aggressive and outspoken, but they look to their dad for a final word." One couple saw this pattern as a result of personality: "Father is quieter and more reserved, but the children respect him and seek his counsel. They understand and respect his nature, but this may have been a problem for them at times, just as the mother's nature has been at times."

As with other activities that foster family unity, talking is a planned activity, arranged for and encouraged even when it's inconvenient. "Our talking is mostly at bedtime or after every sensible person should be asleep," says one father wryly. In one Utah family where two of the married children live out of state, weekly long-distance phone calls are part of the family budget.

One self-employed businessman routinely puts in long days and sometimes has to work weekends, but every week "he takes one child at a time with him to the office and takes him or her out to lunch. And he talks with them before they go to bed."

Several couples, who articulate the value of spending time with each child individually, have set up formal mechanisms to be sure it happens. One couple reports, "This means setting aside time with each child to talk, discuss, do something together, and help them learn in their own areas of interest." Monthly father-child interviews seem to be effective, and no one complained that they seemed stilted or unnatural. "I talk with each child about what has happened during the month, review any problems, give encouragement, and set goals," said one father. "I like being able to have time that I can't be 'squeezed out' of," said another. One set of Utah parents, whose seventh child is eighteen, wished the ideas of personal interviews with each child had been around when their children were younger. "We would have started it at a very young age," they said.

Several of the couples mentioned "monitoring" to catch problems early and then spending extra time with the troubled child. One couple said, "We try as much as possible to interact with each child and watch for special needs very carefully. The children interact with each other a great deal and will handle some situations between them, but when they have special needs, they come to us." The parents of an Idaho family who own a farm equipment business consciously included their ten children in the family business, "worked together, and talked as we worked. If we noticed something amiss, we took time to be with that child alone."

At least two families have consciously taken advantage of contact times to turn them into conversation times. One Idaho couple commented, "The fact that our drapery business is in our home and we are close to schools was a special help. The kids come home one or two at a time, and Mom and Dad are both there to listen to the events of the day. We are do-it-yourselfers, and there are lots of talking opportunities as we work together. The kids work with their dad on the car and home upkeep and repair, and with Mom on cleaning, canning, and sewing. When we help the kids with their projects, we talk. Gathering for prayers night and morning usually winds up in a gab session unless we are under time pressures. After meals, we wind up visiting for sometimes an hour after we are through eating. Whenever a question arises, we look it up in one of our reference books and share it with the family. We save jokes to bring to the family or read each other sections of books we're reading, then talk about it."

A second set of parents observed, "Our most meaningful talks have been in the car, going to and from music lessons, ball games, and so on, and also after children come home from dates and parties. It always pays to be waiting up to share in their joys or sorrows."

38

THE EXTENDED FAMILY

While popular literature might portray each family as somewhat isolated from any kin network, some studies done on families in Detroit in the 1960s show an active and healthy pattern of interaction among extended families. Mormon families also are "plugged into" family networks. For most of the effective families in this study, grandparents, aunts, uncles, and cousins are an important part of their own family unity. Only five families, 2.5 percent, said they were "seldom" involved with the extended family. In some cases, long distances from other family members made visiting a rare occurrence, while several other families had no close living relatives. Out of the remaining families, 51 percent responded "always" to the question: "We are involved in family activities with our extended family." Forty-four percent answered this question "usually" or "sometimes," 2.5 said "seldom," and the remainder did not answer the question.

Three-fourths of these families would "always" or "usually" attend family reunions. In contrast, a study in progress by Phil of college students in western Canada and the Midwest shows that only 10 percent of their families attend reunions. Forty percent specifically mentioned that for vacations, they would visit relatives, either as the main purpose of a trip or as part of a trip. One couple explained that they tried to plan their vacations to include seing a "new place," either a Church-history site like Winter Quarters, some natural feature like Yellowstone Park, or a site connected with national history like Mount Rushmore.

A Utah family with nine children joins the extended family for a week's camping at Yellowstone, a tradition that has now lasted for thirty-five years. When asked to list their three greatest strengths as a family, the first was love, the second was a sense of stewardship for talents, and the third was "being supported and valued by members of our extended family on both sides."

One Utah couple, the parents of ten children, all but two of them married, writes a monthly letter summarizing events from their journals. Not only do the children get a copy but so do their own brothers, sisters, and parents.

One family of four in Utah, with easy access to relatives on both sides of the family, noted, "When more than a week goes by that we haven't seen grandparents, aunts, uncles, and cousins, our children begin to ask, 'When are we going to see Grandma and Grandpa' or 'When are they coming to see us?' Thirty of us are generally together *at least* once a month and sometimes every week. We celebrate each birthday and aniversary, and we often get together for no special reason."

Possibly as a result of this kind of attention, relatives were most frequently listed as family heroes after Spencer W. Kimball (president of the Church when the survey was administered) and several other Church figures. Relatives easily outranked sports figures, popular entertainers, or politicians as heroes. One couple said, "We all follow BYU sports and identify with various sports figures. But the children look up to their grandparents more than anyone else. They were strong, exceptional people. Even our married children talk about them and their ideals." Another couple with five married children said, "We admire a son-in-law who has had a lot of adversity."

The intergenerational impact of family members on family solidarity might make a rewarding study in itself. A family that can supply its own heroes communicates a sense of clan specialness that makes belonging to the family something to be proud of. Family heroes constantly reinforce the notion of "our family," "my grandparents," "my father," or "my cousin" for the children. One family who had a relative listed in *Who's Who in America* was very proud of it, showed the entry to a lot of people, and reminded the children of it. It was not so much an individual accomplishment as a family achievement.

CONCLUSION

We didn't actually tabulate the number of times the phrase "spend time" appeared in the answers to the questionnaire. Our impression is that every set of parents used it at least three or four times. Its sheer repetitiveness impressed us. Parenthood is expensive—time-costly. We've heard a great deal about "quality time" in parenting in recent years; and certainly there's a great deal to be said for intelligent intervention and deliberately planned interaction. However, the 200 families in our survey, although they never used the phrase or talked about it directly, would probably be advocates for "quantity time" as well. They spent time working with their children, talking with their children, being with their children, and teaching their children.

On the whole, we'd have to say that one of the reasons they have united families, bound by commonly shared gospel values and intense love, has to be the sheer number of hours they've put into building those high-quality relationships with each other. "No one else has a higher investment in these children," these parents seem to say, "and there's nothing else we value so much."

Chapter Four

DISCIPLINE: FEW RULES, HIGH EXPECTATIONS

None of the highly effective couples in our survey would say that their family is perfect. As one mother said, "We find there are problems in every phase of our lives. We just get through one set and find another. It is literally that the ultimate test of a 'good' family is to be able to endure to the end."

However it is also true that, at least during the time that the survey was conducted, other people felt that these parents were doing an effective job of rearing their children.

How do these parents get their children to do what they want them to? Do they have strict rules? Do they demand obedience to rules? Do they check on and control their children closely? The answer is no to all of these questions. One of the patterns that stands out for almost every family is they have a few (but specific) rules for children. Even more important than the rules, however, are the expectations. They're high. They're clear. And they have a profound influence on the behavior of the children.

Expectations are a major part of what constitutes the "culture" of family. They represent a general set of unofficial guidelines and standards that everyone in the family understands and accepts, but few families could give you a comprehensive list. As one teenager in such a family said: "I remember when one of my friends was over to our house on a Saturday night and asked if I would like to go to a movie with him on Sunday afternoon. Of course I said no, and he wanted to know why. He asked me if that was one of our rules. As I thought about it, it suddenly dawned on me that it *was* one of our rules except that no one had ever told me the rule that I could remember. There are just a lot of things that our family does different from some others I know, but we just have come to expect the differences and think that is the best way to do things."

Another teenager in a highly effective family told of going home with a friend and showing his father his straight-A report card. The father smiled, gave his son a pat on the shoulder, and said, "Good job, son. I'm proud of you." The friend was dumbfounded. Later he told the son, "Your dad saw all those A's and told you that you had done a good job. I took my card to our dad and it was A's and B's and he was so delighted that he let me put my own phone in my room." The son with the straight A's came from a family where good grades were expected. All of the children were expected to go to school every day, do all of their homework, and get grades consistent with their abilities. This son had always received straight A's and it was routinely expected that he would continue to do so.

In the survey, we asked each family some questions about rules, discipline, and motivation:

1. How many rules do you have for your children?

2. List what you consider to be the most important rules you have as a family.

3. How do you discipline your children? (We offered the choices of positive reinforcement, spanking, grounding, withdrawal of privileges, scolding, talking with them, giving them a "talking to," and "other." We also asked them to rank these discipline measures by how important they were in the family.)

4. How do the children generally respond to your discipline attempts?

5. What kinds of things do you apply discipline for?

6. How strict is your family compared with other families that you know?

7. Do you reward your children for some things? If yes, what rewards do you use? (We offered the choices of

money, trips, TV time, praise, permission to do favorite activities, and "other.")

8. Which of these rewards has produced the best results for you?

9. What kinds of behavior do you give rewards for? (We offered the choices of practicing music lessons, giving talks, getting good grades, going to church, doing non-routine work, and "other.")

10. What are the things that your children *must* do? (We offered the choices of going to meetings, helping around the house, going to school every day, obeying Church standards, living the Word of Wisdom, taking part in family prayer, saving for missions, practicing music lessons, and "other.")

HOW MANY RULES?

Nearly 50 percent of the families indicated they had from zero to five rules, and another 31 percent said they had between six and ten rules. This means that 80 percent of these families felt they had fewer then ten rules. Several families commented that they had many important and high expectations in the family but almost no rules, indicating that a rule represented something more formal than expectations. One Utah couple with five children did not give a number and said, "Our 'rules' are habit and are not itemized." In contrast, one Utah couple conscientiously gave up counting after twenty and said, "We have more than twenty. They must be well understood for a large family to function and feel comfortable in their roles." Another family reflected the same frustration with the assignment by quipping, "We've never really counted our rules. They so quickly become habits which become ways of life!"

Often rules were written down, usually discussed and identified as "one of the rules in our family." Whether written down or not, all family members generally understood what constitutes a "family rule."

One of the most interesting findings came, however,

when we asked parents to identify their three most important rules. The three most common rules were:

1. *You must treat every member of the family with respect.* Over 60 percent of the families had this rule. This meant no verbal or physical abuse, no name calling or hurtful comments, and no fighting. An especially serious violation of the rule was to talk back to the parents—especially to the mother. Few children ever dared to talk back to their father, and usually it was the father who insisted that the children be respectful to their mother. One Wyoming ranching couple with six children reported: "We have this rule—'Thou shalt not hassle thy Mother. Period.' Dad's rule number 1." A related aspect was "good language," and some families resorted to the old but effective "washing out the mouth with soap" penalty for infractions.

2. *You must tell us where you are going and when you will be back.* Fifty-four percent of the families had this rule. Although this rule tended to relax as the children got older, a surprising number of the parents who mentioned it had curfews or check-in times for any children living at home of whatever age. A variation is the rule of a Washington family with four children that "No matter what, we get a phone call if they're going to be later than they'd planned." Another family had no set curfew, but the children were required to wake up the parents when they returned.

Some families indicated that this rule became something of a sore spot between parents and older children, particularly when these children (especially boys) came home from missions. The returned missionary often wanted to be allowed to come and go from the home at will while the parents still wanted to know where the son was going and when he would be back. That had always been the rule, and the parents wanted the rule to still be in force, but now the sons felt that they were adults and that the rules should no longer apply.

Parents, by requiring to know the whereabouts of the children, are in effect saying to the child, "We love you and want to know that you will be all right." This requirement also implies that the child will not be at the wrong place and doing the wrong thing. One mother had a rule that the children must come in after dates and kiss her good night before they went to bed. Not only could she be sure that they were home safe, but it gave her a chance to talk about anything really important that had happened. Also, she noted, "I think that the children were not tempted with Word of Wisdom problems because they knew that when they kissed me good night I would be in a pretty good position to smell any deviation."

3. *You should be a person of integrity, especially being dependable and honest.* Nearly 50 percent of the families had some form of this rule. Many parents said that they explained it to their children in this way: "If you accept an assignment, you should be dependable and fulfill it." "If people are counting on you, you must fulfill whatever obligation it is, even if you don't enjoy it." "You are expected to be honest—to tell the truth, to not lie, cheat, or steal." Many families reported at least one incident of a child stealing something at an early age. The parents would insist that the child make it right. "Each one of our children has taken something from a store when they were young," said one Idaho couple with ten children. "We took each one back, had them apologize to the store owner, and had them work to pay it off. We've never had to do this more than once for any child." Church activity, with assignments to give a talk, attend a meeting, or accept an assignment, came under this dependability rule as well.

These families were large, busy, and hard-working. The parents clearly needed some assurance that their children would be where they said they'd be and do what they said they'd do. One farm couple explained, "If we left the kids with the milking, we just assumed that it would get done. The milking has to be done, and there is no room for any kind of excuse. They know that if they are detained somewhere for some important reason, they had better get in touch with some of the neighbors and have them start the milking."

Several parents also had firm rules about the use of private property. Some said that if one child used another person's belongings without asking permission, the matter would be discussed in family council and a penalty decided there.

In addition to these three rules, shared by over half of the families, came another cluster of three rules shared by about 25 percent. First was the rule that each child had to do his or her share of the work. Some families wrote out weekly lists of chores each person was to do, while others simply had "understood" assignments. Many farm families, for instance, tended to assign more of the outside chores to the sons while daughters concentrated on helping their mother with the household tasks. Other families assigned chores more or less by age, with one child inheriting a task from an older sibling when he or she became old enough to do it. Still other parents simply assigned the children jobs on the basis of whatever needed to be done, but they frequently reminded them, "Remember, everyone is supposed to do his or her fair share."

Teaching children to work, assigning work fairly within the home, and launching children into the larger world of work is certainly too complicated to be dispatched by a couple of rules. Chapter 7 discusses the topic in greater detail.

A second rule shared by 25 percent of the families was the requirement to treat the home with respect. This usually meant that children were not to break things, "roughhouse," or be careless with property that would be expensive to replace or that had sentimental value. One rebellious teenager deliberately flouted this rule by making greasy footprints on the carpet.

The third rule, which about 25 percent of the families said they had made explicit for their children, was living Church standards. This rule covered a multitude of activities: not dating until sixteen, participating in family prayer and family home evening, not swearing, paying tithing, and reading the scriptures. A Utah Valley couple with six children observed dryly, "It is a rule to obey the rules." However, nearly all of the families indicated in one way or another that adherence to Church standards was an expectation, more fundamental and pervasive than rules.

DISCIPLINE

Of course, children sometimes break rules, and the parents must then decide what to do about it. From a long-term perspective, a rule serves a function even if a child persists in defying it. A child who knows that the family standard forbids smoking, for example, may experiment with smoking during the growing-up years, but the clear standard of right and wrong is there. He uses that rule as a measure of his own conduct, and it generally serves as a constraint and eventually as a motivation in helping him change.

When we asked parents to identify the disciplinary measure they used with their children, this was the order:

1. Positive reinforcement. Eight-five percent of the parents listed this method as their first or second choice. Most of them felt that by identifying the behavior they wanted and praising the child for it, they reduced the probability of bad behavior later which they would then have to punish or try to correct. One set of parents observed, "When we tell our son how well he is doing, he just beams all over, and we know that he will work hard to do that same thing in the future. He really runs on praise. As parents, we can sure tell you that it is a lot more fun to praise than spank."

2. Talking *with* the child (a calm discussion of right and wrong) was listed by 97 percent of the parents. One father wrote: "I try to teach my children correct principles so they can see what is right and wrong behavior, and hopefully they will be able to govern themselves. When one does something we feel is wrong I try to sit down with the child

and ask the child if he or she understands why I am upset and why we are having this talk. I then try to get the child to see why it was wrong and to get him or her to agree to improve in the future."

3. Sixty-six percent of the parents used withdrawal of privileges, such as not being able to watch a favorite television program, go to a friend's house, or stay up late for a special event.

4. Forty-five percent would give the child a "talking to." It would be interesting to know if children make a distinction between "talking with" and "being talked to," but most parents did. In this second case, more intense emotions were involved, there is less concern with having a discussion, and more emphasis on the parent talking. One child described it as "laying down the law."

5. Grounding. Forty-eight percent of the parents said that for serious disobedience by older children and teenagers, they would withdraw permission for the child to date, visit friends, or use the car. They were required not to leave the home except for school and necessary meetings for a certain period.

6. Scolding. In this scale of disciplinary measures, parents seemed to see scolding as the angriest form of communication they had with their children. Yelling, threats, perhaps name-calling occurred; and many parents indicated that they lost their tempers. Some admitted saying things they later regretted. Only 55 percent said they used it while 45 percent said they did not. One father told us, "I scold the children at times, but mostly it grows out of my own frustration. If things aren't going well for my wife and me, we sometimes take it out on the kids. Sometimes they deserve it, though."

7. Spanking. This was the only form of physical punishment on our list of suggested disciplines, and it was the last measure listed. It was also last by a rather wide margin: 45 percent of these parents, many of whose children had been small during a much less permissive period of child-rearing, said they had never spanked. Only 3 per-

cent of the families indicated that spanking is their first discipline measure, and 9 percent list it as the second most important measure for them. Many families noted that it was age specific—that they stopped spanking about age five or age eight. One family specified that it would spank until about age twelve, and no one explicitly said that they still spanked teenagers.

Still, in evaluating the highly controversial measure of spanking, it is interesting that 12 percent of these highly effective families see spanking as either first or second in importance in disciplining their children. Since these children seem to have turned out to be successful and effective, spanking does not seem to have been disruptive and alienating, particularly in the way it was done. One father described his spanking sessions this way: "I spanked my little children seldom, but it was serious. I would use a belt and it hurt. I also don't think I ever spanked any of my children as they got close to being a teenager. However, after a child had received a spanking, I think I honestly tried to follow the scriptural admonition to "show forth afterwards an increase of love." I would hold the child in my lap and hug and kiss him or her and tell that child I loved him or her. Then I would talk with that child about why I had given the spanking, and we would try to come to an agreement about avoiding problems in the future."

One of the fathers in our sample recalled something of his own growing-up years and remembers being spanked: "I got spanked a lot—more than I do my own children. You know, the interesting thing about it is that I can never remember my dad spanking me when I was not at fault. Oh, I didn't like it at all, but even at that time I knew I had it coming. Now that I am older I can really say that all of the spankings did me good. We don't spank that much, though. Probably my wife has had more influence on better discipline than I."

Philosophically, some parents use spanking as a last resort, when everything else seems to have been ineffective.

One son said about a spanking from his father: "Dad didn't spank any of us children very often, but when he did, we knew it was about something Dad felt very strongly about. It didn't take us kids long to learn what would get us a licking from Dad!" Still other parents used it on a serious first offense, particularly with little children, to teach them the seriousness of it.

It would be interesting to probe this element a little more. Did some parents who would not spank a child on the bottom slap him or her? How did the children see spankings? And how, for that matter, did the children perceive their parents' measures? Were they as aware of positive reinforcement as they were of groundings or spankings?

Still, the data from this research is clear. Almost all of the parents tried to control their anger in disciplining children and hence avoided the most emotionally intense forms of scoldings and spankings. Instead, they seem to have used preventative discipline—first by teaching correct behavior and reinforcing it, then by using an escalating scale of communicating with the child—discussing, withdrawal of privileges, and so on. "And sometimes," sighed the parents of nine ranging from five to twenty-one, "you try everything and nothing works. Sometimes success is just a matter of the right combination of the child, the day, and the situation."

Many parents who added "other" forms of discipline agreed with the Utah parents of eight who listed "natural and logical consequences." Another frequently applied form of discipline was sending the offending children to their rooms. The Utah parents of six found that waiting up for late teenagers was very effective because "they hated it." The Wyoming parents of five children would use additional chores as an incentive for obedience. Another family found that "reasoning together" was their most effective method of discipline.

REASONS FOR DISCIPLINING

When we asked parents to identify the reasons they would apply discipline, they gave these reasons in order of frequency of occurrence:

1. The child disobeys the parent's direct instructions to do or not do something, or violates one of the family's rules, expectations, or norms.

2. The child comes in later than agreed.

3. The child fights with siblings.

4. The child does not do assigned work.

5. The child treats parents or other family members with disrespect.

There is considerable overlap between these reasons. Most families would agree that doing assigned chores and not fighting would be family rules; but obviously obedience and responsibility are high values in all of these families. One parent said, "I feel that children should 'honor their father and mother,' and when they do not obey our requests I feel this is not honoring us." Many couples listed specific infractions that had triggered a discipline "clamp-down": sassing, stealing, and jumping on the beds. One couple said they punished their thirteen-year-old for unauthorized joy-riding in the family car.

In an area so value-laden as discipline and one in which advice from child-rearing experts has changed conspicuously and often within two generations, many parents sometimes flounder and feel confused. In an interview, parents in one of the less-effective families mused, "If we could start over again, we would make up more rules. The kids have always done what they wanted to, and we thought that they would make the best choices, but they didn't, and now it is too late. Of course, we haven't done so well with the choices we made either." A father in a less-effective family stated, "My dad used a belt on me, and I think I turned out okay. It's the kids who don't get belted that end up in reform schools. They just run wild, and the parents don't line them up." A mother in a less-effective family commented somewhat wistfully, "Our standards are too high, I think. With our oldest children we get after them for not getting all A's on their report card. We never do tell them that they are doing well, even when they get better grades than most of their friends." Still another set of less-effective parents was completely frank about their motives in discipline: "We send them to their room a lot, and that gets them out of our hair and away from each other."

The highly effective families in our study were not immune from confusion and fatigue, but they seem to have thought through some of the issues more thoroughly and carefully. They also seem to have behaved more consistently. Many of them wrote illuminating comments about their philosophy of discipline. A Texas mother of four wrote: "When they were too small to reason with, we sometimes used spanking, but generally only when they were endangering themselves or someone else. When our oldest was about seven years old, a neighbor asked me how often I spanked him. I honestly couldn't recall the last time I'd had to spank him! In general, we have found that Joseph Smith's method worked best for us: Teach them correct principles and they govern themselves.

"I think the three oldest were probably all in grade school when we had a family council where they helped make the family rules and also determined what the punishments would be for breaking them. The rules included such things as (1) Be on time for dinner, (2) Let Mom or Dad know where you are going, (3) Bed made before school, and so on. They chose the penalties, and often they were more severe than we would have imposed. During the council meeting, we sometimes had to temper the penalties a bit. We didn't want penalties we weren't willing to enforce!

"We tried to help the children choose natural consequences. For example, the penalty for not making one's bed was to have to sleep on the floor the following night. The penalty for not checking out with Mom or Dad was being grounded for a period of time. Being late for dinner meant no dinner. The interesting thing about this whole plan was that they imposed punishment and really helped us enforce it with each other. When we might have been tempted to 'go soft' on one of them, the pressure from the others wouldn't allow it. 'Ha, ha, you sleep on the floor to-night!' was usually met with good-natured embarrass-ment. The first night of floor sleeping may have been fun, but it soon wore off.

"We asked our daughter about this method of disci-pline the other day, and her comment was, 'We just knew if we didn't do right, you'd be *so disappointed* in us, and we didn't want that.'

"Not all children would respond to this method in the way ours have, and perhaps we have not really been tested as parents. My grandmother used to say she wouldn't know what kind of parent she had been until she saw how her grandchildren turned out. She was training not only children but the next generation of parents! Too few young couples set out on the sea of matrimony with so large a view of their destination."

"In our family," echoed one set of Idaho parents with four children, "we did not use discipline so much as we al-lowed children to suffer the consequences of their own ac-tions, without too much interference. If they stayed out late, they still had to get up early and go to work."

Another couple wrote, "We have felt it important that our children learn to complete assignments at an accept-able level. We try to follow up on every assignment to see if it was done and how it was done." They passed over si-lently the level of self-discipline such consistency requires of parents.

One Texas couple "always resolve contention im-mediately," they wrote. "We never let a child go to his or her room angry and let pouting make the problem larger." This couple also felt strongly that children shouldn't be "bribed for good behavior"; and instead of offering re-wards for good behavior, they tried to create an atmos-phere with an "abundance of love where all the children could express their feelings, even angry ones, knowing that we loved and accepted them. We tried to have reasonable expectations but then tried to be absolutely consistent. Needless to say, we weren't always great at the consistency part." When their children pointed to other children who were rewarded for good behavior, these parents explained the principle behind their action: "In this life, rewards don't always come to deserving people. We need to learn to do right because it's right, not for any other reason. Only our Father in heaven will always reward us. Trust him."

These parents used physical punishment to teach acceptable behavior at a very young age. If a child threw a tantrum in public, an immediate spanking in public followed. If one daughter (their four oldest were girls) bit another, the mother bit back, explaining that the daughter needed to know how it hurt and cuddling her until she was comforted, then asking her if she understood about making a different choice the next time. The parents decided that, at about the age of eight months, their children were old enough to be quiet in church, and each child got a "bare-bottomed spanking" for misbehaving, followed by explanation and loving. "With five of the children, it took only one experience. With one it took two. And with one it took five," the mother recalled. "All of our discipline is based on 'reproving betimes with sharpness'—perhaps not always moved upon by the Holy Ghost—then showing forth afterwards an increase of love, explaining, talking, and loving."

The mother wrote that as a result of this early and thorough training, "I could take our children anywhere and be proud. We called them our angels while we heard other parents referring to theirs as monsters and beasts. It's true that some of those children seemed hyper, rowdy, and snoopy. Perhaps because our expectations were clear and our discipline was consistent, we knew we could depend on ours." Furthermore, she said, "our girls have been such a good example for our [three younger] boys that we've never had any trouble with them."

Some parents focused on making the discipline itself a

learning experience. "When we discipline we ask our children to pray about the situation and listen to what the Holy Spirit tells them to do," wrote the Utah parents of nine. "Thus they are disciplined by a higher source than us, and by themselves." In answer to a question later in the survey about the three most important rules, the mother wrote, "Follow the Spirit! Follow the Spirit! Follow the Spirit. The children can always recognize it, for it encourages them to do good and gives them a joyous, peaceful feeling."

Another family reinforced agency by letting the children choose between two punishments or choose their own. A Utah couple with seven children ranging in age from five to twenty checked all the forms of discipline except spanking as "number one" and explained, "The most important thing is that they know the price of their unacceptable behavior before the transgression. Then the form is really irrelevant." Still another set of Utah parents explained, "We have a high degree of trust that our eight children will make the right choices. We are generally tolerant of errors and treat them as errors rather than as a sign of badness."

One mother reflected ruefully, "We have not been strong disciplinarians. We didn't know how to be. But I was against hitting or spanking." In another family, the couple had decided before they were married, "Our children will never own a car of their own until after marriage or mission. They would be privileged to use the family car when necessary and as they deserved to do so. We have never had a problem with discipline and cars with any of our nine children (six boys). We attribute this to making our decision and sticking to it."

Most parents would probably agree about the importance of consistency: "We feel it is very important for parents to stick together on discipline whether they agree at the time or not." Another set of parents corroborated, "By being firm and not changing the discipline, we grew closer together." In a Utah family with seven children, the parents saw their discipline styles as very different. The mother did most of it, using positive reinforcement first with talking second, and "not making an issue" out of rebellion but instead finding "another way to give the children the responsibility for their actions." The father was stricter about most things and tended to begin discipline with a "talking to," but both agreed that they were more relaxed parents with the younger four than with the older three, and the wife felt good about supporting the father's discipline, even when she didn't agree with it.

Consistency did not necessarily mean sameness. Several parents acknowledged the differences between their children: "Some of our children were very sensitive to heart-to-heart talks," said one mother. "Others sometimes required a loss of privileges to get their attention." Another couple observed that "our oldest often shuts us out. The other two are very attentive and have shown no signs of rebellion." In one Idaho family where the father had been married four times (the first three wives had died, leaving several small children each, and the fourth wife brought eight children of her own to the marriage), the parents had a firm rule for themselves in imposing discipline of "never comparing children or what they do or do not do."

One couple wrote: "Our children have all been different from one another in many ways. A couple of them didn't seem to respond to discussions, and we had to spank them occasionally. Others we would talk to and they would just seem to understand and were willing to do what was right. One son would become very difficult and obstinate unless we found something to praise him for. A little good, honest praise would make him work all the harder to make sure that he would get praised again. As he grew older, we didn't have to praise him so much. He just got better in all areas, it seemed. We think we would praise more and spank much less if we were starting all over again with little tykes."

The parents also revealed their own efforts at self-discipline in dealing with their children. "We always endeavor to be fair," said one couple. "We feel it is important to listen to them to know where they are coming from." Their own commitment to listen defused anger and hence curtailed "explosive" disciplines. Another couple also set controls for themselves: "We tried not to discipline in front of other people. We learned early that if the kids were humiliated, even the best form of discipline would be ineffective." One father said, "I would spank only occasionally, and then I'd send them to find a stick while I collected my thoughts and feelings and evaluated them."

CHILDREN'S RESPONSE TO DISCIPLINE

In an attempt to determine effectiveness, we asked parents, "How do your children generally respond to your discipline attempts?" Three-fourths (76 percent) of them said that their children generally accepted it. One couple said that "closer relationships and mutual respect" resulted from their discipline. An older couple, the parents of seven, expressed a sense of reassurance about the choices they had made: "Good, sound, constructive, consistent, loving discipline has actually built a bond between us and each of these children. You want them to be their best because you love them. We feel we have been on the right track with our disciplining, because all four of our married children are using basically the same methods."

Other parents said that their children basically accepted the discipline but that acceptance was not infrequently preceded by resistance or waiting, a "testing it out" or "thinking it over" period, but that usually the child ended up agreeing with the parents.

A minority of parents reported compliance with the desired behavior after discipline but in such an angry and resentful mood that it ended up being a generally negative experience. "Pouting" was a problem with some of their eight children, confessed one Utah couple. The Idaho parents of four boys recall a consistent pattern of the children "arguing, debating, reasoning, and finally submitting" while the parents reciprocated by listening, reasoning with them, accepting their reasons as valid when they could, and negotiating more satisfactory solutions when they felt their children had a good point. About 20 percent said that they could not give one answer for all their children because some accepted discipline while others rejected it.

It is interesting that even in these effective families, 5 percent of the parents reported that the general response to their discipline was rejection. Usually teenagers seemed to feel this way, certainly one of the reasons why many parents feel teenagers are the hardest to rear.

COMPARATIVE STRICTNESS

When parents were asked, "How strict are you in your family compared with other families you know?" the results were:

Much stricter	17%
Somewhat stricter	54%
About the same	17%
Less strict	10%
Much less strict	2%

Since each family compared itself to other families they know, there is no way of knowing if there is any common standard of strictness. It is quite possible that in some areas "grounding" a child could be seen as being very strict, while in another community "grounding" is a standard practice and only spanking a child or giving an angry scolding would be considered strict.

It is also possible that strictness is seen as consistency of discipline. A strict family, by this definition, would be one that *always* applies discipline for an infraction. A less strict family would be one that would overlook infractions much of the time and only occasionally apply discipline. One parent put it this way: "I don't think we are a very strict family—at least when I compare our family with the way my dad handled us kids in my parents' home. But when I watch the way many of the children of our friends behave, I am astonished. We just would not allow our children to act

that way. I see kids talking back to their parents, arguing—
almost fighting, refusing point-blank to obey, staying out
late without thinking of calling home, never seeming to do
any work around the house—well, we just would not accept that kind of behavior. So in comparison, I guess we are
stricter. But we didn't have to talk about it to discipline the
children because nobody did certain things. They especially didn't sass us. We had high expectations that everyone understood and met, but certainly we were not a rule-
regulated family. We had a lot of freedom and flexibility,
and as I look back on it, our children seldom abused the
freedom we allowed."

A Provo, Utah, couple with three girls and four boys
wrote: "From a strong base of commitment to each other
and the gospel, a strong family is able to be very flexible
about rules, patterns of life, and interactions with each
other and the community. We feel that the love and nurturing the children get during their earliest years is critical in
building that foundation. In our family, the mother was
constantly available for preschool children because that
was crucial, we felt, to their development. We also feel that
having a sense of humor and not taking ourselves or each
other too seriously has enabled us to enjoy each other and
build a bond that enables us to be happy."

A California wife with four living daughters wrote
somewhat with mingled apology and pride: "My husband's partriarchal blessing says that the children who
would come into our family would be choice spirits and
they have been. I'm afraid the Lord would not trust us with
any of his problem children. Our girls have just naturally
seemed to want to do right. My husband's remarkable
sense of humor has done much to make our home a happy
place."

A Salt Lake City father with eight children observed,
"We're strict when it counts, yet we allow a lot of discre-
tion. If we take a stand, we follow through to enforce it;
however, we do not take stands lightly." Another couple
explained, "Our family standards are higher than average

but perceived discipline is less because family members generally do not need strictness."

"MUST-DO" REQUIREMENTS

We asked parents, "What are the things your children *must* do?" In addition to checking off the kinds of things they required from their children, many families wrote this kind of comment: "In our family there are very few things our children *must* do in the sense we absolutely require it. Particularly as our children get to the age of eight, we feel they have their free agency and should have the right to choose." Another wrote: "The word 'must' on your questionnaire is too strong for us. We do not make them do anything, but rely on the principle of free agency. Our children know that we use a pretty hefty amount of persuasion, though. We strongly encourage a lot of things but don't *make* them do anything in the final analysis." "We don't insist or force them to do any of these activities," wrote the Utah parents of nine, "but we encourage them to do all of them. They choose for themselves." A California couple with six children ran an eye over the list and admitted, "These are all 'musts' with room for exceptions—and there have always been plenty of them."

However, most families felt that they had strong enough expectations that there was a sense of "must do" for the following activities:

1.	Go to church	76%
2.	Help around the house	89%
3.	Go to school every day	94%
4.	Obey Church standards	82%
5.	Live the Word of Wisdom	82%
6.	Take part in family prayer	78%
7.	Save for a mission	49%
8.	Practice music lessons	51%

Among the "other" must-do's listed here were working hard, saving money for their own needs and wants, speaking respectfully to parents, and respecting the rights of others.

It is interesting to note that going to school is significantly ahead of the next-nearest activity, helping around the house. Going to school is also a legal requirement, and most parents feel they cannot let their children make a choice to stay home. Interestingly enough, one of the less-effective families felt that "our kids have to go to school every day unless we have something better to do. School isn't the only place to get an education, and we take them out a lot and do other things like skiing and fishing." While many effective families would agree that "school isn't the only place to get an education," probably very few of them would agree that recreation would be more important than school or agree with the rule-flouting attitude expressed in "unless we have something better to do." All of these effective families expect their children to take rules seriously—family rules, Church principles, and law.

MOTIVATIONS AND REWARDS

While discipline is sometimes seen as the negative, controlling side of child-rearing, positive attempts usually have the same end in mind: to increase desired behavior and reduce unwanted behavior. We also asked some questions about this area so that we could make some appraisals of which factors seemed most effective.

We first asked parents, "Do you reward your children for some things?" Eighty-seven percent said yes; 13 percent said no. We then had them go over a list of rewards:

1. Praise	88%
2. Permission to do something special	72%
3. Money	43%
4. Trips	18%
5. TV time	10%
6. Other	11%

Parents jotted down such items as treats, special clothes, sports equipment, notes of appreciation, and "trusting them with real responsibility."

The rewards that were seen as most effective and producing the best results were praise (57 percent) and permission to do something special (15 percent). The Idaho parents of six explained that a real reward was "allowing them more freedom to do things they wished to do when they learn responsibility. They have usually chosen good things." One Utah mother of seven cheerfully confessed, "I usually give money when I'm too tired to be creative and think of a reward that will build character."

"Love and approval is the reward they get, and they appreciate it," said a significant number of parents.

"We did not set up an award system," said one couple. "We just gave what we had at the time. Sometimes it was a special meal or dessert. Other times it would be a rose, a treat, or a note left on a pillow or put on a plate."

"We would contract for a reward for something accomplished," said other parents. "Our three sons achieved the Eagle rank. We agreed to pay half on a shotgun if they completed their Eagle. With another child, we agreed to get contact lenses if she finished reading the Doctrine and Covenants by age fourteen."

Several parents expressed concern about the "bribery" aspects of a rewards system, even though one couple frankly listed it among the "other" forms of discipline they used. One widowed Salt Lake City mother of five said: "I've always felt that rewards as such were not the best system. Children should do many things for the simple reward of accomplishment. We expect good grades and praise them, but we don't bribe our children to get them. We might want to do things together after we've worked hard together on a project, but we don't hold up the reward of a movie or money as an incentive. When the children were little, perhaps we'd go out for ice cream or make cookies—something that particular child would especially enjoy—but we never decided on a reward ahead of time. We've tried to identify their feelings of joy when they've done something and praise *that,* make *that* the reward."

Another Salt Lake couple who adopted ten children use rewards in a combination of system and spontaneity. They keep party-favor surprises in a "treat bowl," and a youngster who manages to do something right that he's been struggling with gets to pick one out. Other rewards are a night out alone with Mom and Dad, or a pizza party for the family. "Often," says this mother, "we give a reward just for love—because we just love the children and want to do something special for them."

Parents most frequently rewarded these actions:

1. Non-routine work (special achievements)   55%
2. Good grades   52%
3. Something that comes up we want our
   children to do   27%
4. Practicing music lessons   24%
5. Giving a talk   20%

"Other" rewarded behavior included "no cavities," advancement in Scouting, "doing their best in their activities—concerts, ball games, or competitions," and compassionate service.

A Texas couple with four children wrote: "Many of our children's friends have been rewarded for good grades with $1 or $5 for each A. We have never felt this was a healthy approach. One of the best rewards we have found has been a family celebration. When one of the children brought home especially good grades, we took the whole family out to dinner to celebrate. It is good reinforcement when an older brother brags about how his younger brother's good grades are the source of a pleasant experience for the whole family, and we all look forward to the next grade period. Praise and rejoicing together over each others' accomplishments has been our best reward technique."

One Utah Valley couple take their four sons out to dinner every quarter to celebrate good grades—but it's not a reward. They've never had low grades. In one Utah family with seven children, giving talks, getting good grades, and going to church are "expected—therefore no material rewards are given." Probably other parents would also agree. "We tend to give rewards spontaneously, after the fact," said one couple. "We don't routinely hand out rewards in an attempt to foster improved behavior." Even here, however, flexibility paid off. With one child, money was the most successful motivation for achieving a goal.

Often the parents would plan how the reward system was going to work and make it correspond with the goals they set, within the framework of their family values. "We really use the rewards in diverse ways for each family member," wrote one couple. "As we talk together, we discuss each child and try to come up with something that will help him or her move in the proper direction. For one it may be a reward to get her to work on her music, as we think she has a pretty good talent with that. For others it is a reward to help them pick up their grades a little bit. Sometimes the children complain when another child gets a reward that they would like, but we tend to ignore that. The children have been told that we try to personalize the rewards to help them do better, and they know that in the end they all about even out."

CONCLUSION

These effective Mormon families have high expectations, a few rules, and usually a struggle, whether they use positive or negative means to obtain compliance. We asked two of our final questions to see how well parents thought they had done. They were to check the appropriate blank: (1) "In general, we think our family is____very special,____ about average for the families we know, or____not as good as most families we know." (2) "How does your family compare with your own ideals and expectations for your family?"

Eighty-nine percent of the parents checked the "very special" place on the first question; 10 percent checked "about average for the families we know"; and only 1 percent checked "not as good as most families we know."

In answer to the second question, 75 percent of these parents said that their families met their expectations. Twenty-three percent said that their family fell "somewhat short of our expectations." But only 1 percent responded that it fell "very short" of their expectations. (One percent did not respond.) One of the couples who checked the second answer, a family with seven children, had seen two of them divorced and two fail to graduate from high school. They commented: "I think as a family we've learned that the principle of free agency is very important; and when you reject it, you're taking a course that will afterwards bring some sorrow. However, as a family we've learned about unconditional love and caring and never giving up. We're not the typical wonderful family that boasts of every child a missionary and all married in the temple, but we've had enough adversity to help us be compassionate to others in difficulties (there are a lot of them in the Church) and enough of seeing children change to give us hope. We've learned that life is always going to be a test. There's never a time when you are through with the hard things and can relax."

Chapter Five

PARENTS AS TEACHERS: GOSPEL TEACHINGS AND SECULAR EDUCATION

Several of the parents in our study cited the well-known quotation from Joseph Smith about his method of governing the Saints: "I teach them correct principles and they govern themselves." The Lord has assigned parents the responsibility to teach their children, and these parents accept it. Another favorite quotation is: "Inasmuch as parents have children in Zion, or in any of her stakes which are organized, that teach them not to understand the doctrine of repentance, faith in Christ the Son of the living God, and of baptism and the gift of the Holy Ghost by the laying on of the hands, when eight years old, the sin be upon the heads of the parents." (D&C 68:25.)

LDS children, to some extent, live in two worlds: the gospel-centered world of the Church and the achievement-oriented world of secular society. Sometimes these two worlds are seen as compatible, sometimes not. The family and Church classes are the primary means of instruction about the first world. Public education is the primary means of instruction about the second. The effective parents in this study consider themselves responsible in both spheres to help their children succeed.

We asked a cluster of questions designed to show what parents do in both areas:

1. How do you teach your children? (We offered: talk to them regularly, try to set a good example, hold regular family home evenings, read scriptures together regularly, and "other.")

2. About how many hours per week do each of you (include only the children at home) watch television?

3. How many hours each week do you watch television together?

4. Do you control what programs the children can watch?

5. Which Church magazines do you subscribe to?

6. How many of you in the family usually read at least half of the *Ensign, New Era*, and *Friend?*

7. What kinds of books do you have in your home? (We offered "a lot" of Church books, "a few" Church books, literature books, dictionary, encyclopedia, history books, atlas, biographies, "other.")

TEACHING ACTIVITIES

We asked parents, "How do you teach your children?" Here are the responses:

1. Try to set a good example	100%
2. Talk to them regularly	94%
3. Try to hold family night regularly	63%
4. Read scriptures together regularly	34%
5. Other: look for teaching moments, encourage reading Church books	20%

Many parents added explanations about the top two methods, clearly the favored and, they felt, their most effective teaching methods. "When we go out to build fences or work with the machinery, we talk together as father and sons," said one ranching father. "Sometimes we talk about the gospel and my mission. Sometimes we talk about political issues and things that are happening in the world. And sometimes we just work."

Ninety-nine percent of the parents said they always pay their tithing; 97 percent always attend Church meetings; and 93 percent always accept Church callings and assignments. Furthermore, 97 percent of them said they actively try to help neighbors who need it, with the result that the children see a model of rendering service to others. Over 98.8 percent of these couples were married in the temple or were sealed there after a civil wedding. Both father and mother have a personal commitment to education (80 percent of the fathers and 70 percent of the mothers had attended college). They are very active in fulfilling Church callings, and they emphasize the importance of the family by the amount of time they spend with their children. Clearly, as far as modeling Church commitment is concerned, they expect to be their children's primary models.

Sixty-six percent of the families said they hold a weekly family home evening "usually" or "always," but only 28 percent say they "usually" or "always" read the scriptures regularly. From this, we infer that the parents do most of their teaching in informal settings.

Actually, this is quite logical. Family home evening is only once a week, but informal talks or discussions seem to occur almost every day. When we asked parents what they did regularly together in the family, this is how they responded:

1. Talk together   always 64% usually 31%
2. Do things together   always 61% usually 35%
3. Do household chores
   together   always 32% usually 40%
4. Discuss family problems
   together   always 52% usually 40%

These families see themselves as spending considerable time together talking, discussing problems, and doing things together. Doing household chores together is lower than we might have thought; but at least one family from Idaho listed "working together" as one of their most effective teaching techniques, while a Utah Valley couple with five children "always worked with the children on household or yard chores to teach them properly." One Utah couple with seven children ranging in age from eighteen to thirty-three recalled, "We not only have always played and prayed together, but we have had some of our best teaching moments *working* as a family."

Several parents included examples of the kinds of values they taught. "Sometimes in our prayers we will address a specific problem and ask for divine guidance in helping to understand or cope with a situation," one couple observed. The working out of the problem then constitutes a built-in basis for discussion. "We have used important events in the extended family as times for discussions; for example, mission farewells and homecomings, temple marriages, blessings, baptisms, Scouting advancements, and family reunions," say another couple.

An Idaho couple with ten closely spaced children remain alert to "take advantage of the teaching moments that come daily. Whenever questions arise, we go to our reference books and find an answer." They also have lively mealtime conversations dealing with current events and recent lessons from Church and school classes.

Similarly, another couple has formed the practice of talking "with our children about the lessons they have been given in Seminary, Primary, Sunday School, and so on. A common table topic at dinner is 'what did you talk about in your class today?'"

"Often we will take a certain person (Church leader, current-event figure) and talk about that person and look at what we can learn (either positive or negative) from their example," said the parents of another family. "Sometimes we will just talk about the good things in the lives of those who live around us."

A Texas couple and their four children have a tradition of "piling on the parents' bed and talking—making plans, sharing ideas, setting goals, swapping experiences. . . . That's probably our best teaching technique." A Montana biologist and his wife found that the family council with their four children was an effective place to teach. A Utah couple worked consciously to ensure that their eight children "have good [then crossed it out and wrote "growing"] experiences inside and outside the house."

One Wyoming couple with six children gave them responsibility "at an early age and then held them accountable." They commented that this was one of their most effective teaching devices.

SCHOOL

We asked parents in our sample about their own schooling. Husbands averaged 16.0 years—coming out to exactly four years of college—and wives averaged 13.8, or almost two years of college. When we asked them to appraise their own children's scholastic performance, about 66 percent reported that their children had above-average grades. (The breakdown for the children by birth order was that 64 percent of the first-born children earned "above average grades," with second children coming in at 67 percent, third children at 66 percent, and fourth children at 65 percent.)

One couple said, "We try to talk with our children's teachers to see how they are doing and what we can do in the home to support what the teacher is trying to get across." They did this with the children's Primary, priesthood, and MIA classes as well. One Salt Lake City family with five children, the father a technician and the mother a secretary, have made academics a high priority. They have "one Sterling Scholar, one nominee, and one working for it" among their children.

One mother of four, who said her children were "very easy to teach" and had "never given us worry or heartaches," observed, "Our children have not been leaders in student government or high achievers such as Sterling Scholars, though they have all averaged high grades in school and received several scholarships."

READING AND TELEVISION

We asked our parents to identify their reading and television habits for two reasons: we wanted to get at some of the attitudes they had toward education (and reading is usually a fundamental) and also to see how they handled the potentially controversial problem of television.

More than two-thirds of the highly effective parents felt that their home libraries were above average in the neighborhood. The breakdown looks like this:

1. Much better than most neighbors   34%
2. Better than most neighbors   35%
3. About the same as most neighbors   26%

One Utah mother of five, who checked "better than most" observed in the margin. "We're always loaning books."

What kinds of books do the families have in a home library? Almost every home has a dictionary and an encyclopedia, and about 80 percent have an atlas. In these homes, Church books occupy an important place—99 percent said the home library included "a lot" of such volumes. Literature—novels, poetry, adventure, Westerns, science fiction, and essays—appeared in about 80 percent of the libraries, followed by history and biography in two-thirds of the home libraries. Parents also mentioned cookbooks, game and joke books, "how-to" books, foreign-language books, children's books, and books dealing with science, Scouting, politics, business, art, music, and special fields. Some families also mentioned "heavy" traffic in and out of the public library, or made a comment like, "We read *a lot.*" One Utah couple with a professor father and college-graduate mother checked everything and then jotted down, "We have tons of books of all kinds."

Church magazines formed a good share of the reading. Ninety-two percent of the families took the *Ensign,* and 46 percent read at least half of the magazine. (Only 2 percent "never read" up to half.) Eighty-four percent of the families took the *New Era,* and 52 percent read at least half. (Only 3 percent "never read" at least half.) Forty-three percent of the families took the *Friend*—probably reflecting the age distribution of the children—and 41 percent read at least half. (Only 5 percent "never read" half.) Besides Church magazines (several couples also listed such Mormon-oriented publications as *This People* and *Church News*), the average family also subscribed to four other publications. Most frequently mentioned were *National Geographic, Time* or *Newsweek, Reader's Digest,* and *Better Homes and Gardens.* Many homes would also include a specialty publication connected with the father's work (*Chemical Engineer, Money*) a special interest of the parents (*Farm Journal Workbasket, Golf Digest, NEA Journal*), and some other magazine geared to the interests of the children, such as *Popular Mechanics, Boy's Life, Sports Illustrated, Byte, Compute!* or *Seventeen.*

One Montana family with a contractor father, homemaker mother, and only two of six children still at home (boys fifteen and seven) subscribed to all three Church magazines as well as *Reader's Digest, Smithsonian, National Geographic, U.S. News & World Report, Hot Rod, Oceans, Montana Outdoor, Church News, World, Ladies Home Journal, McCall's, Better Homes and Gardens, Freeman,* and *Prevention.* A Utah family with seven children subscribes to more than twenty magazines, including two on pigeon racing and five on horse racing. Additionally, almost all the families interviewed reported that they subscribed to a daily newspaper. Our study did not ask who in the family read what or how much, but the evidence is clear that parents in these homes had a generous supply of good reading available for the family members.

When it comes to television watching, our sample showed a strikingly low number of hours compared to a national sample. Our study showed that on an average day, the parents and children at home watched for an hour and four mintues. A national survey in 1982 showed almost triple that time: two hours and fifty-one minutes a day median time. (Robert T. Bower, *The Changing Television Audience in America* [New York: Columbia University College, 1985].) When we looked only at the college-educated portion of our sample, they watched only 55 minutes compared to the 1982 national sample of two hours and eighteen minutes. We tried to break the pattern down even further; here's what the data show:

Children between two and five watched twenty-seven hours and nine minutes a week in a sample collected by the Nielsen rating. Our sample watched eight hours and thirty-six minutes. Children between six and eleven from the national sample watched twenty-four hours and fifty minutes while ours watched eleven hours and forty-two minutes. Starting at age twelve, we broke the figures down to see if there were any differences between male and female viewing patterns. Teenage boys in the national sample watched twenty-five hours and seventeen minutes while ours watched nine hours and twenty-four minutes. For girls, the time was almost identical. The national sample watched television for twenty-four hours and sixteen minutes while the teenage girls in our sample watched for nine hours and twenty-nine minutes.

Young adults between eighteen and thirty-four showed an even greater divergence from the national sample. Young men in the national sample watched twenty-eight hours and thirty minutes compared to five hours and fifty-seven minutes in our sample while young women in the national sample watched thirty hours and nineteen minutes compared with our sample of six hours and twenty-two minutes. During the highly productive years of thirty-five to fifty-four, when most adults are juggling the responsibilities of work and rearing their families, the national sample of men watched an average of twenty-seven hours and fifty minutes (compared to our sample of ten hours and eighteen minutes), while the women watched thirty-three hours and twenty-three minutes. The women in our sample actually watched less than the men, with seven hours and twenty-four minutes. The biggest gap, however, occurs in the retirement years. American men over fifty-five watch television an average of thirty-five hours and fifty-three minutes, while our sample was seeing six hours and six minutes; women of the same age were up to forty-one hours and thirteen minutes—the equivalent of a full working week—while women in our sample tuned in their sets an average of six hours and twenty-four minutes. (*Trends in Attitudes Toward Television and Other Media: A Twenty-four Year Report by the Roper Organization.* 5B:84, April 1983; *Public Perceptions of Television and Other Mass Media: A Twenty-Year Review, 1959-1967: A Report by the Roper Organization*, April 1979.)

Thus, in our sample of highly effective families, most of the television viewing was done by the children between six and eleven by an impressively large margin, while young adults watched the least amount of television. At most, however, members of highly effective families are watching less than half the national average number of hours and, at the point of widest divergence, only one-eighth as much. About 5 percent of the parents we surveyed said they did not watch television at all during the week. One Utah family with six children from ten to twenty-five logged barely an hour's viewing time a day for everyone except for the seventeen-year-old, who had medical problems and whose viewing was about ten hours a week.

In general, watching television together is not an important activity that the family does together. Fifty-four percent of the families said they watched television together as a family two hours or less a week. One Washington family with six children explained, "We do not watch television often because we find other activities, especially reading, more interesting." Another 37 percent said they watched less than ten hours a week as a family. The Provo parents of nine wrote: "When our twins were asked what their favorite television show was, on a school survey, they wrote 'The News.' They were eight years old. This was probably because we all watch the news together and discuss the day's events."

One mother observed, "Sometimes we watch television as a family, and sometimes I listen to it a little as background noise when I am home alone doing the ironing or other work. I seldom ever really look at it, however. About the only thing that we consistently watch is the news and the Choir broadcast on some Sundays." (Several women mentioned having the television on as "background" while they did housework.)

When we asked parents if they controlled what their children watched, they answered:

1.	Always	24%
2.	Often	38%
3.	Sometimes	21%
4.	Seldom	10%
5.	Never	7%

However, the matter of control means different things to different people. One Provo family of five commented that the television had always gone off after supper until homework was finished, unless an exceptional program was on. One father said: "We don't check up on what programs our kids watch. However, we have talked about television programming, and our children know the kinds of programs we don't approve of. Since we can't check every program they watch (and don't want to), we feel we must tell our children our standards of television programming and trust them to control their own television watching."

A Wyoming couple commented, "Our family seems to choose good programs. If we comment that a show is unfit or if the children see material that they know is not appropriate, they don't watch it."

A Wyoming forest ranger and his wife do not monitor what their children watch, but they have decided against cable television, and they screen the videos the children are allowed to watch. A Provo couple with seven children seldom control programming: "We suggest; they choose," is the way they put it.

Although our study did not probe this area particularly, the comments of the parents who wrote them indicated that they had thought through how they wanted their children to relate to television—whatever it was—and felt comfortable with it. In contrast, one of the less-effective families indicated dissatisfaction but vagueness: "Our kids watch way too much television. I guess we shouldn't let them do it like they do."

CULTURAL EXPOSURE

One couple wrote, "We have read to our children extensively from birth, and we talk about what we have read. We have used books and observation to learn about trees, flowers, birds, animals, and a whole range of subjects."

Another couple corroborated, "It is important to us that our children learn something about the elements of good culture. We have tried to have good music and paintings in the home. We keep books and have a recommended reading list. Then we take our children to concerts, plays, seminars." "When we travel or even on short trips, we try to visit places of interest," said one couple. "We have gone to historical places of interest to the Church or the country. We may visit a museum, an art gallery, a beautiful building or natural setting." A couple of families have reading lists of suggested books, or find books on interesting topics that come up. In a Utah family with seven children, the piano-teacher mother wrote: "We started at an early age to steer our kids toward appreciating better music and away from rock. We feel terrific about how they respond to classical music."

In one Provo family of seven where the father is a professor and composer and the mother is a homemaker and student, the family works together on reports and projects. The children "have had many hours of reading from their mother," and they take walks together. "We sustain excitement about learning and accomplishments," they wrote. In another family of seven, also from Provo, the parents deliberately include good music and great paintings as part of the home environment.

Music lessons, as a reflection of family culture, came in

77

for a high share of comments. Several parents commented that they had tried rewarding their children for practicing, often unsuccessfully. Another couple required that the children pay the teacher, but then paid the children for practicing, a rather ingenious rule. Another family had the rule that "every child must learn something about music. He or she can choose the instrument to play, but must be involved in music lessons and practice for two years. After that they can choose to continue or stop."

An Idaho farm couple with four sons and three daughters observed that practicing music lessons was not only expected and required but "needed rewards" to really work.

CONCLUSION

Although family educational goals in our survey differed from family to family, a general pattern is clear. Highly effective parents feel comfortable in their role as their children's teachers, whether that involves giving them the skills, structure, and discipline they need to succeed in school; explaining and implementing gospel principles; consciously exposing them to important cultural elements; or reinforcing the children's own learning efforts. They consider themselves responsible for and they are responsible about helping their children become well educated. They also consider themselves to be the primary conveyors of religious values.

Chapter Six

SHOWING
AFFECTION

Because love has always been part of the pattern of happy family life, and since the parents in this survey ranked it with gospel commitment as one of two important elements in their successful family life, we wanted to know more about what that meant.

Do loving families express love verbally? By hugs? By kisses? By doing kind things for each other? Do they always treat each other with respect? At one point Christ said to his disciples, "If ye love me, keep my commandments." (John 14:15.) Should we expect to find more obedience in families where members say they love each other? The Doctrine and Covenants (121:41-43) says that power and influence should only be exercised by "love unfeigned," and that if reproof is given, it should be followed by an "increase of love." How do highly effective couples teach family love to their children?

We asked:

1. How do you express love in your family? (We offered: tell them, hugging, kissing, doing things for one another, writing or telephoning, providing a living for, or "other.")

2. Please rank these ways of expressing love with 1 being most important.

While the data gathered may not give us complete answers to all of our questions, it is possible to identify certain trends:

1. Tell them we love them   97%
2. Do things for them   96%
3. Hugging   94%
4. Tell by writing or phoning   91%
5. Kissing   85%
6. Provide a living for them   74%

Answers in the "other" slot semed to cluster in a couple of major areas:

Getting together, talking,
   sharing, supporting   72%
Teasing and joking   20%

We also asked parents to rank in order the various expressions of love and to indicate which they did first, second, third, and so on. The findings show the following as the actions they took first or second:

1. Telling   62% first   24% second
2. Doing things for   40% first   33% second
3. Hugging   17% first   24% second
4. Kissing   12% first   7% second
5. Write or phone   12% first   7% second
6. Provide for   8% first   12% second

These families indicated that "telling"—either face-to-face, on the phone, or in writing is most important, followed next by "doing things" for a loved one, and then by touching.

As this tabulation shows, 94 percent of the families indicated that hugging was a part of family expressions of love, and 85 percent said that kissing was. Still, it seems that there are some good families that have little or no physical expressions of love and affection. Both hugs and kisses were among the top seven, but they were not at the top, and they were only two of the top. Hugging was the most popular form of physical affection mentioned, with kissing occurring 10 percent less often. About 17 percent said that kissing would be the last method for showing love, and 7 percent said that hugging would be last.

It is not possible to tell what constitutes a hug or a kiss in these families. When we asked people to be more descriptive during interviews, we got definitions of a hug that ranged from a two-armed, full-body embrace to putting an arm around the shoulders. Kissing might be a generous smack on the lips or a peck on the cheek. Some families have a pattern of kissing openly. Bishop H. Burke Peterson, formerly a counselor in the Presiding Bishopric, and his brothers have a habit of kissing each other on the lips whenever they meet. This pattern would be absolutely foreign to many other equally good families. President Spencer W. Kimball was almost legendary for his overflowing love, which manifested itself (outside his family as well as inside it) with a kiss on the cheek, an affectionate hug, or holding the hand of someone he was talking to.

It would be interesting to check perceptions with the children in our sample to see if they felt love being communicated as the parents meant to communicate it. One mother, who indicated that "doing things" for her children was a primary mode of showing affection, commented, "I don't think my children will ever appreciate how much we love them and how much we sacrificed and did for them until they have children of their own. When they are up all night with a sick child, frantic with fear, or when they go to work the next day heavy with fatigue, or when they spend the few dollars on toys for the kids rather than something for the parents—maybe then they will remember that we did all of the same things for them." Perhaps she is right, and perceptions of behavior as love will develop more over time.

None of the survey responses suggested that affection was not important. One Utah couple with four children checked everything and wrote in the margin, "This is what it's all about!" An Idaho farming couple with seven children wrote, "These are all important. Our family has needed them all depending on age and circumstances." The Provo mother of nine children explained that "the boys wrestle with their father in a fun way," but she added, "All the forms of affection are interrelated. You can't have one without the other. We do feel it is *very* important to express our love for each other often."

One Utah father of five, four of the children sons, had deliberately patterned physical affection into the family structure. He wrote: "I think we're an affectionate family—at least, we hug and kiss a lot as family members come and go and at special events. When our children were young, we gave them lots of physical affection; but as the boys got older, they seemed somewhat embarrassed if we kissed them, especially in front of their friends. I tended to back off a little, although their mother still kissed them. It was nice to have a daughter, because she *liked* to be hugged and kissed and I enjoyed doing it. But I didn't like never touching my boys either, and I found they liked it when I'd sneak up behind them and grab them in a big bear hug or start a mock tussle. Later, I decided to kiss them as I left on a trip and returned—or if they were going somewhere. I talked with them about it; and aside from the initial awkwardness of starting the custom, it has become an accepted family practice. We still do it, and all of the children are married now."

Many parents wrote comments that showed their family had created a "family definition" of love. One Utah family added that they showed love by "forgiving." Another Utah couple wrote: "Love is service to one another, feeling or showing that you care through actions, showing interest in and involvement in each of their individual activities, interests, projects, and friends." An Idaho family with ten children also had little family traditions of "winking across the room, holding hands, or blowing a kiss." Another Idaho family added "honoring birthdays, family jokes, and stories" to the list of how they showed affection, while "being together" and "talking to them with respect and appreciation" was tops on other families' lists. A Utah couple with seven children also added "pats, backrubs, teasing, horseplay, and special family home evenings to honor someone." A Texas couple with four children simply said, "Surprises!"

Traditionally, parenting has meant providing. We included the question about providing a living to see how strong this belief still was. Some parents were puzzled by it and jotted down an explanatory note that the children were "on their own now" or that "this went without saying." One of the less-effective fathers, interestingly enough, responded to it directly by saying, "We don't show any affection in our family. Oh, I think that we love each other most of the time, but we just don't show it. I guess just making a living for the children ought to be an expression of love for them. Lots of families don't even provide for themselves." A Provo couple indicated that they showed love by "providing educational opportunities" for their children and "going places together."

One mother said, "I do many things out of love for my children. I will fix a meal early or make a lunch when they have to go to work. I will iron a dress or shirt, provide refreshments for a party, pick up after them if they are busy. I feel I do many things for my children because I love them. But I am not always sure they recognize what I have done or if they really appreciate it."

When we did follow-up interviews with some families, we found differences in the ease and openness families felt in expressing love. Several of the questionnaires had indicated some inhibition about physical affection. In one California family, the parents hugged and kissed, but one child did not like to be kissed.

More frequently, it was the mother and father who had different feelings about hugs and kisses. One mother said, "The father by nature is not a hugger or a kisser." In one family, the parents indicated that neither hugs nor kisses were part of their affectional repertoire and explained, "We're just not the type." Both parents had grown up in home where physical affection was not common, but they had found other ways to communicate affection for their children. In a follow-up interview, they agreed that there was a lot of love in the home but that "it gets expressed in other ways."

Some couples indicated that a common way of expressing love was "me too" response. If one member of the family were to tell another that she loved them, the other's response would be to say "me too." In some families, it seems difficult to freely say, "I really love and appreciate you." The interviews also revealed that in some families the most open expressions of love and appreciation came through the public forum of ward testimony meetings. Often a husband or wife could more easily express deep feelings of love and appreciation in a meeting than in a private, face-to-face encounter. One reason may be that there would be no possibility of rejection or interruption during the meeting; and while a child might feel squirmy or embarrassed, he or she would not feel required to respond in some way when the parent had finished. The public setting thus, in a way, becomes a method of safeguarding privacy. Children also used this public form to express feelings of tenderness and appreciation that they might otherwise have kept to themselves. More than one couple said, "The first time I heard our son say he loved us was at his missionary farewell."

We also asked parents how often members of their family showed physical affection to one another. The results were:

1. Daily   81%
2. Weekly   9%
3. Monthly   2%
4. Never   1%

Since this question did not ask couples to specify which form of affection was used on these occasions, it could range from a hug or a kiss to a pat on the back, a touch, or a routine greeting or goodnight kiss. It could also include a warmly affectionate conversation with horseplay or lots of hugs.

In a family's life span, the pattern of showing affection seems to undergo some development. We have a general impression that the American culture shows kissing and hugging as commonplace in most families when children are young but decreasing as children get older. It also seems somewhat more culturally acceptable for daughters to continue to kiss both parents than for boys. A son now forty, who was interviewed during the follow-up phase, recalled the pattern in his family of thirteen children: "When I was small my parents would always kiss me, but as I grew older my mother would kiss me, but father did only on special occasions, like when I went into the military service. Then as I got older I had left home, of course, and I would always kiss both of my parents when I saw them. My sisters did all along, but I don't think that any of the other brothers did."

Most families indicated that they "of course" hugged and kissed an adult child on landmark occasions: when he or she left for college or on a long trip, at a wedding, at graduation, or at a time of special recognition. They also responded this way when a child was ill or emotionally upset, no matter what his or her age.

It seems remarkable that so basic an area of family interaction has never been studied with a national sample, but there is simply no data available for comparison. A recent study of BYU students shows very little physical affection expressed between fathers and sons, except when the sons are very small, although there is rather more between fathers and daughters. It seems logical to expect some generational differences to develop, with families of the future being more openly affectionate. The new emphasis in the nation as well as in the Church on involving fathers more actively in the actual work of caring for infants and toddlers may make them feel more comfortable about continuing to hug and kiss them as they grow.

Certainly, the absence of ways to express physical affection appropriately must be related in some way to the shocking rates of father-daughter incest in this country and the widely publicized correlation (though not necessarily a cause) between homosexual men and emotionally aloof fathers. Some serious family specialists have encouraged more appropriate physical affection between dads and boys, dads and daughters, and other members of the family. There is no way to measure the tragedy of normal, healthy affection between parents and offspring that must manifest itself in joyless, abnormal, and even violent ways.

Chapter Seven

CHORES, WORK, AND MONEY

We asked families to identify activities "that you consider to be very important in your family and that family members usually have a strong interest in doing." Here are the top items for activities strongly centered inside the family:

1. Travel   77%
2. Playing musical instruments   75%
3. Sports (outside of school)   74%
4. Parties in the home   67%
5. Sewing   60%
6. Singing in the home   50%
7. Hobbies   41%
8. Fishing and hunting   40%

Besides these activities, we also asked parents to identify what the children did outside the family. They reported:

1. Boy or Girl Scouts   85%
2. Earning money outside the home   83%
3. Sports in school   75%
4. Academic interests   74%
5. Playing musical instruments   71%
6. Going to dances   71%
7. Having dates   70%
8. Speaking in public or debating   56%
9. Holding office in school   53%

10. Singing in public   51%
11. Parties outside the home   48%
12. Being in plays or drama   44%

Families also added such recreational activities as watching videotapes, camping, working on art projects, canoeing, horseback riding and horse racing, swimming, picnicking, hiking, visiting family and friends, reading good books together, and watching family movies and slides.

In one Salt Lake City family, the eldest daughter of the five children cuts everyone else's hair. A Utah couple mentioned a family project of "appreciating our American heritage and freedom," but they did not explain how they carried it out. One Utah family with two boys and two girls did a lot of boating, water skiing, and "forever feeding friends. Our kids always brought their friends here, even when they were small." Another Utah family with eight children finds that "guests" are a major family activity: "We have lived in a number of places," the couple explained, "and our list of friends is long. We have overnight guests very often, and children from the families of friends stay a number of weeks at a time in the summer." An Idaho family with ten children, five of them married, regularly gets together on Sunday evenings to make and show home movies. Another Idaho family of ten has a "game closet filled with games and puzzles and a large dining-room table where we gather regularly to play."

It was interesting that the second-most important reason why children were not home was that they were employed. Usually, it was not poverty that drove them to work. When we asked these families to rate their income as above, about the same, or below that of their neighbors, 60 percent of them checked the "above" box. A more important reason is that these highly effective parents have a strong work ethic. They teach their children good work habits, encourage them to work, and want them to experience the satisfaction of earning their own money. One mother reported, "All of our children have been expected to work around the house even when they were small. As they got older, we didn't actually force them to get a summer job or to work on Saturdays or after school, but all of the children knew that they would have a lot more money to spend if they earned it than if they always came to us for a handout."

How did these parents pass on work values? And how did they handle the problems involved in getting children to do their share of the household chores? We asked:

1. Have your children obtained jobs outside the family while they were still living at home?
2. If you require your children to work around the home, how much time, on the average, do you require each week for the following ages? ____5-10 years; ____11-15 years; ____16-20 years; ____21-25 years.
3. Which kinds of jobs do your girls do? [We offered a list that included yard work, dishes, cleaning, work in the garden or on the farm, work with animals, help with canning, help with cooking, fixing the house, fixing the automobile, and "other."]
4. Do you have family projects? [We listed gardening, genealogy, memorizing poetry or scriptures, building/remodeling/adding on to the house, working in the family business, doing missionary work, service projects, and "other."]
5. Do you give your children an allowance?
6. Do you require your children to work for money they get from you?
7. About how many dollars per week do you give your children at 6-10 years? $____ 11-15 years? $____ 16-20 years? $____; 21 and over but not married? $____.
8. Do you help your married children in any of these ways? money as gifts, money as loans, child care while they work, occasional babysitting, advice, blessings, "other."

In answering the question about requiring household chores, 77 percent of the parents responded that children did at least some of the household chores on the list. A surprisingly high 60 percent said that children did these chores willingly. One family of five headed by a lieutenant colonel in the army added conscientiously, "Most of the time," and a Utah father of seven penned in, "Sometimes. Kids are kids." A Utah couple with five children added, "We never expect them to do something we would not do ourselves," and a Utah couple with eight children acknowledged, "Our children are above average in their attitude, but they did not always do household chores without occasional feelings of unfairness."

We had asked an earlier question about "the things that your children *must* do." Although many of the parents rephrased the question in terms of expectations rather than requirements, almost 90 percent said that helping with the family chores is an expectation in the family. Thus, the expectation is about 15 percent higher than the children who actually *do* work.

One mother explained the problem this way: "We have tried to get our kids to help around the house, and we have tried everything—restricting TV, paying for work done, grounding, scolding—but nothing has worked for very long. The kids get busy, and I find it really easier to do it myself that to get into a hassle with the children."

One Provo father of six recalls the chore/allowance intersection as a consistent frustration: "This was always a bugaboo for us. We tried every scheme imaginable to get our children to work in the home, and nothing was too successful. TV was used as a reward, and that worked for a time. We tried putting out a list of jobs in the home with the amount to be earned for each task. That just didn't work. The children said they didn't need money when we needed work done. We finally came to the point that we provided money as it was needed and tried to get agreements with each child as to that child's fair share of the family work. It's some comfort now to discover that many other good families struggle through the same issue. My wife has also found out that she isn't the only mother who moved in and silently did a child's chores when she felt that the child was struggling with a heavy schedule or a problem with a friend. But we were probably too lenient in requiring work around the house. If a child was busy in some other legitimate activity, we nearly always excused him or her from the chores."

We asked parents how much time they expected children to work each week around the home. Here are the results by the ages of children, the *average* time expected, and the *most frequently* listed time. This third listing is important. For example, for ages five to ten, most families expect only two hours of work a week. However, some families, usually farm families, expect much more, so the average is much higher—four hours a week.

Age	*Average Hours of Work Expected per Week*	*Expected by Most Families*
5-10 years	4 hours	2 hours
11-15 years	7 hours	4 hours
16-20 years	9 hours	4 and 10 hours
21-28 years	11 hours	2 hours

The group of children between sixteen and twenty actually has two points—four and ten hours. Again, the difference is clearly related to where the family lives. Urban children who have a heavy schedule of academics, sports, other lessons, recreation, and easily accessible friends are expected to work at home only four hours a week. Rural families with the demands of crops and animals to care for required more hours of work from their children and usually checked ten hours. One farm mother explained, "Our children have always been willing to assist with the home and farm work. Most of the families in the community seem to have about the same pattern. Everyone works. Some, of course, seem to let their children get by with doing less, but our whole community works and seems to believe in it. As we have watched the children get older and leave home, we see the most success from those who had responsibility and had to work. Work is just part of life."

The reports on children ages twenty-one to twenty-five still living at home are too varied to produce a common pattern. Only forty-five families out of the 200 still had children of that age living at home. Usually, missions, work, school, or marriage have taken them away. In some of the families, children in this age group had almost complete responsibility for taking care of the home. Others working full time had almost no chores. Thus, our data rather misleadingly shows that the average amount of time expected for this older group is eleven hours a week, but the time most frequently checked is two hours. One mother whose twenty-three-year-old son was living at home and working full time said: "Now that he is working full time, we expect very little from him in helping around the house. In fact, we would be delighted if he would just make his bed and keep his own room picked up. He is a great young man (returned missionary) and we want him to save his money and get married, so we do not charge him room and board. I don't think he realizes how much additional work he creates. He thinks since he is gone to work all day and out most evenings that he doesn't have much impact in the home. But I still do his laundry, fix his meals, make his lunch, and pick up after him and his friends when they are here. There is a lot more work than he thinks."

A substantial number of parents jotted down explanatory comments about how much or how little their children worked, at what, and how willingly:

"In our family there was no set number of hours children were expected to work each week. Everyone was expected to pitch in, and we all kept the house neat and clean. The house is cleaned for the day before everyone leaves for school or work. We have breakfast together, family prayer, and sometimes scripture reading."

"The amount of time children work at home is difficult to measure," observed one Provo couple with nine children ranging from nine to twenty-two. "In the summertime, those at home work one to four hours per day. As they get older, they get jobs away from home and they spend less time working at home."

One Utah couple doesn't give their fourteen children allowances or pay them for working. They said, "We want our children to learn how to work in the family without feeling, 'What will you give me for it?' or 'How much is it worth?'" They also required a substantial amount of work from their children: seven hours for children under ten, ten hours for children under fifteen, and twelve hours for children between sixteen and twenty.

"In our family each person is responsible for some personal things—room and clothes,"wrote another couple. "Then we usually all work together until what we need to do is finished."

One couple controlled the amount of time spent in work because they wanted the children to do other things: "We had a bulletin board with the jobs each person was assigned to do after school. We varied jobs from time to time so one person didn't always do the same thing. But once the children finished their work, we did not add to the list. They need time for some play and homework." In another family, academic interests and doing well in school were extremely important to the parents. "To provide study time for six children, we gave them a break at home—so Mother did more of the work than in many families," they wrote.

A Salt Lake City family with seven living children took a middle position. "All of our children have delivered the paper from age eight. This has always provided them with their spending money until they choose to earn more," wrote their mother. "But we think that their senior year is soon enough to work at more than odd jobs. Too much money too soon makes them too independent when they are not always wise. There's a time for everything; and we want them to enjoy and learn during high school—not earn." This same family also puts a limit on housework: They clean one floor of their two-story house on Thursday and the other story on Friday. Then they use Saturday as a "fun day."

Interestingly, a mother in one of the less-effective families commented, "Our kids are all involved in the farm, but the kids hate it because their dad is a workaholic." The term, "workaholic" did not appear in any of the discussions about work among the highly effective families.

"MEN'S WORK" AND "WOMEN'S WORK"

We wondered how traditional these highly effective families might be and if strict gender roles were part of the family pattern. For that reason, we asked parents which chores boys did and which chores girls did. Interestingly enough, most of these homes showed a very egalitarian approach to work:

Job	Girls Only	Boys Only	Both
1. Yard work	4%	23%	71%
2. Doing dishes	23%	2%	76%
3. House cleaning	21%	1%	77%
4. Work in garden or farm	4%	18%	78%
5. Work with animals	4%	21%	75%
6. Cooking	42%	2%	55%
7. Fixing the house	8%	40%	52%
8. Fixing the car	1%	86%	13%

Out of all of these activities, only "fixing the car" is clearly seen as men's work. For all of the rest, over half of the responses indicate that the activity is considered appropriate for both boys and girls. One Idaho couple with three children wrote down "sewing and mending" as another activity and said that it was required of their two boys as well as their daughter. Other families specified that child care was required of both boys and girls, while a Provo family of seven also involved both sons and daughters in grocery shopping, typing, doing the laundry, and "balancing the checkbook."

The responses indicated preferences for girls doing dishes, house cleaning, and cooking, while boys more often did yard work, farm or garden work, animal care, or fix-it projects. But it is possible to see in this pattern an emphasis that getting the work done—not who does it—is the important value.

Some of the comments parents added indicated an unconscious awareness of gender in the family's work patterns. "As long as our children lived at home, they made their own beds and kept their rooms straight," wrote one couple. "The boys took out the garbage and did the yards. The girls helped with meals and general housework. Sometimes they would have to fit these chores into their schedules, so jobs were not always done at the same time."

One Texas family with four daughters followed by three sons checked everything in duplicate, then commented: "No sex discrimination here. We feel it is vital for everyone to know how to perform all these tasks. The girls gas cars. Mom takes it in for repairs. The boys cook and clean."

FAMILY PROJECTS

We also wondered if these effective families encouraged or created family projects, either to increase togetherness or to teach skills. We asked if their projects included a garden; genealogy; memorizing poetry or scriptures; building, remodeling, or adding on to the house; a family business; missionary activities; or service projects. The only projects that received a significant number of answers were:

1. Family garden   74%
2. Some service projects   58%
3. Building or adding on to the home   48%
4. Family business   47%

Forty-four families distributed their answers among the rest of the choices.

About three-fourths of the families had a garden, but it was not clear that all of the family members worked in the garden. Some families responded that the whole family helped prepare the plot and plant the seeds, but the up-keep fell on the mother or father or perhaps one child. A service project would often occur once or twice a year: Sub-for-Santa, taking a basket to a needy family for Christmas, helping a widow clean her yard, or doing something special for a family with an illness or some other special need.

MONEY

As discussed in chapter 4 in the section on motivation, 43 percent of the families used money as a reward for behavior they wanted to celebrate or encourage, but this figure was low compared with 88 percent for praise and 72 percent with permission to do something they particularly wanted.

Money in our society represents independence, but it can come to people in two ways: as a gift motivated either by the recipient's need or the giver's generosity or as earned income, directly related to work.

Allowances

We asked our effective parents about allowances. Their responses showed clearly that there is no one right way to handle money in the family. Forty-three percent of the couples gave their children an allowance, but 57 percent did not. When we asked if the parents required their children to work for the money they gave them, the results were symmetrical. Nine percent said "always" and 9 percent said "never." Thirty-two percent said "most of the time," 13 percent said "often," 25 percent said "sometimes," and 12 percent said "seldom." Thus, equally effective families have very different strategies for dealing with money.

One Utah couple with five children ranging from three to sixteen had an allowance formula: "Twenty cents per week per year of age up to the age of ten. After that, the allowance is based on work completed around the home and yard." One couple gives each child a modest weekly allowance with a healthy bonus: $10 a month if they follow the family guidelines on low-sugar use.

One father tied family money closely to the work ethic, explaining, "We have our children work for what they get. There are too many who grow up expecting things for nothing, and we think we can start at home to avoid this problem. If our children want money, they work for it." One Salt Lake City couple ruled, "Anyone who lived in the home was obligated to help keep it operating"; and when one daughter was going to summer school full-time and could not hold a regular job, they paid her for yard work and cleaning on the apartments they owned. "We feel this is wiser than giving her money," her mother wrote. "It becomes 'her' money, and we have noticed that she spends it more judiciously."

At the other end of the spectrum, a father responded, "There are a lot of things more important than money, although it's certainly significant. We let our kids have what they need and don't require them to work for it per se. Working around the house is just part of being in our family. We do for them what they need and hope that the advantages will pay off in the long run for them."

Among the families that gave allowances, many had set amounts for younger children but provided what was necessary to supplement what the teenagers earned on their own. The families paid weekly allowances in these ranges:

For ages 6-10
$1 a week	76%
$2 a week	14%
over $2 a week	10%

For ages 11-15
$1 a week	52%
$4 through $6	34%
$7 through $10	10%
over $10	4%

For ages 16-20

$1 through $5	57%
$6 through $10	21%
$11 through $20	16%
over $20	6%

Only 14 families out of 200 gave allowances to children twenty-one or over, and then the amounts varied widely. In one case where a daughter lived at home to care for an invalid parent, she received a sort of salary for this service to the family. Many parents also helped their college students by paying tuition and books or by providing room and board while the student worked part time. Some parents also gave a college student a car or helped pay for car expenses as a contribution toward education.

It is also clear from these amounts that the parents were not lavish with their children. Children under ten seldom received more than $2 a week, and children under fifteen received about $5 a week. Since these families usually would not allow dating before age sixteen, we expected to see an increase around that age; but even then, the weekly allowance was less than $10 a week. Many parents said that they provided money as needed for a trip, a special dress, or a prom; and an increasing number of children had part-time jobs of their own. In response to the question "Have your children obtained jobs outside the family while they were still living at home?" 94 percent responded yes; 4 percent responded no.

In some cases, these part-time jobs were seen as contributions to the family income, not as personal income. In other cases, the money belonged exclusively to the child. In one family, the father, a miner, was injured in an accident. "The kids just had to help with things," explained one of the married children. "Each one contributed so much of their babysitting money and then their wages, as they got older, and I don't think any of them regretted it. We all loved Dad so much and were happy to assist as we could. Now that some of us are married, it is a little easier to assist since we make more money, and I know that Mom and Dad appreciate it."

Financial support from the children seemed to be the exception, however. Instead, most of the comments from parents dealt with the thorny problem of allowances. Fifty-seven percent said something like: "No fixed allowances. We gave them what they needed." "We tried an allowance when the children were young," said one couple, "but found with us it was better to give money when they needed something. If they wanted something special, we gave special assignments and had them 'earn' their money. We kept track of their savings and payment of tithing. When they had 'savings,' they could buy things. They would also add to their savings account at the credit union."

Another couple gave regular allowances and required regular chores but said that their children were "allowed to work to earn extra money." Several families used this system. One mother wrote, "Occasionally, if extra money was needed, I would try to find a project—painting, extra yard or housework—that they could do for extra money. Allowances were given regardless of behavior or daily chores done."

One couple with four children wrote: "Our children have had an allowance, mainly to help them learn the principle of tithing and the principle of saving and managing money. When they needed money over and above what their allowance covered, we kept a list posted that included fifty-cent and dollar jobs. They could arrange with us how much extra work they wanted to do, after their regular chores were completed. We used a job chart when they were younger and assigned such chores as cleaning the bathroom and doing the dishes on a rotating basis. As they grew older, we sometimes made a list of jobs that needed doing and let them sign up for two or three they chose. Changing the method occasionally helped make the routine more interesting."

In some cases, payment was in kind. One farm couple

did not try to keep track of how much work the children were required to do, but in exchange "they got a 4-H steer they sold for spending money, missions, and school." During busy seasons like harvest, they would also get wages. In an Idaho ranch family, the three children had to feed their calves before breakfast and catch the 7:30 A.M. bus. Both sons bought a dairy calf and a range calf from their father when they were about 4-H age and received wages for taking care of the calves and also as a percentage of the milk check. They could build their own herd as the animals matured, deciding whether to keep or sell their animals. The daughter also worked on the farm for wages. "She preferred it to housework," her mother commented.

In one Salt Lake City family, all ten children—seven sons and three daughters—had their own paper routes to earn spending money. When the parents needed babysitting, they would hire the older children to do it at $1 an hour, and there were set amounts for some jobs: $5 to wash the car, $5 to mow the lawn, $5 a day for working in the father's accounting business, and so on.

For one couple, the most important value was teaching proper work habits to their children. Paraphrasing the Lord's commandment to Adam to "earn his living by the sweat of his brow," one couple explained: "We have taken it upon ourselves to teach this to our children. A lot of the problems of the world result from people who never learned to be dependable and to work. We go out of our way to find work for our children to do. It is not easy for us, as it was for our parents who lived on farms. When we were young, the jobs never ended; but here in the city, the jobs end sometimes. We scout out work for our children at home and in the neighborhood. There's always someone who is glad to get some yard work done. Our daughters all babysit. The jobs don't always just come. We sometimes have to help the chidren put signs and get the word out that they can babysit. This doesn't relieve them from their regular household duties. When time is short, the kids help each other, and we even help deliver newspapers when our son has to get through in a hurry to get to a special Scout program or something like that. Most of the time, we let him sweat it himself, however."

In a few families, money was not private property. One couple did not give allowances but allowed their children to earn spending money by doing yard work and babysitting at about age ten or twelve. "We function under the idea that since we work as a family, all the money that comes in is for all of the family. The children ask for money when they have a need; if the money is available, they receive the amount needed."

One Utah family with nine children and a disabled father used a "United Order" model. All the money that came in belonged to the whole family. This common fund "paid the bills, sent missionaries, and so on," wrote the mother. "When they needed anything, and if it was a good thing and if it was possible to give it to them, they got it." She praises their financial management: "They do not spend money foolishly. They can have money in their pocket and never spend it if they don't need to."

In one Idaho family with twenty-one children produced in four marriages, each child celebrated his sixteenth birthday by being placed on the family checking account on which he or she could draw with permission.

Still another couple accustomed their eight children to the world of work by paying an hourly wage. With a Montana farm, they found it comparatively simple to work out a regular bookkeeping system: "The children get money only when they work. Up to age ten they earn between a dollar and three dollars an hour. Up to fifteen, they make between two and three-fifty an hour. Between sixteen and twenty, they earn three to four-fifty, and more during harvest—up to $80 a day. Over twenty-one, they earn between four and eight dollars an hour, and they put in long hours." This couple also pointed out that their children are very good at saving most of their summer wages and that the four boys old enough for missions have paid at least half of their own way.

SUPPORT FOR MARRIED CHILDREN

We were also interested to know how the financial arrangements within families changed for married children. Did money seem to be in a different category than supplying emotional support, child-care, and other goods or services? It would be interesting to have comparative national statistics, but the closest available are from a 1983 *Better Homes & Gardens* survey called *What's Happening to American Families*. This survey showed that 56 percent of the parents would let a married child return home to live for a limited time; 21 percent would welcome an adult child back with no reservations; 9 percent would be reluctant; and 6 percent would refuse. Most students of the family generally believe that many people supply money or child-care service for their young married children and also supply money and care for elderly parents. In our sample, 14 percent of the parents tended grandchildren regularly for married children who worked, and an additional 60 percent tended grandchildren occasionally. Sixty-four percent "gave advice" to their married children; 52 percent gave money as gifts; and 50 percent loaned money to married children. We were pleased to see that 60 percent of the fathers gave blessings to their married children on request.

As usual, the comments that had been added were illuminating. A Utah couple with fourteen children helped their four married children build or remodel their homes. Several couples mentioned supplying food to their married children, particularly meat and milk from dairy farms and cattle ranches, fresh fruit and garden produce, bottled fruit, and food-storage items. Car repairs and the loan of a vehicle were also mentioned. A Salt Lake mother of six children, three of them married, made home-sewed clothing for them and the twelve grandchildren. One Wyoming couple have cosigned notes with their two married children.

An Idaho couple have a family partnership on their farm with their two sons; and one son and his family live in the basement apartment where the parents lived as newlyweds. "The partnership makes things somewhat equal," the father wrote. "The farm has paid for everyone's schooling, missions for both sons and our daughter, and individual pay as a living wage every month. Our arrangement is probably unusual. Everyone must work, but we all work together and share, and we consider one another's well-being. We work hard at getting along, too, especially by letting our children discipline and raise their own children."

One Utah couple own a four-plex and have allowed all of their children to live in it rent free at one time or another—"while they were finishing the last year of school or when they were newly married." Still another Utah couple have an "open-door policy on our food-storage in the basement when our married children are hard up." A Salt Lake couple gives each child a quarter-acre of land as he or she marries to build on or sell. Still another Salt Lake City couple usually gives each newlywed couple "a piece or two of furniture from our home."

While all of these effective families have had to work out some system for channeling money to their children, they usually do not directly buy good behavior with it. Parents give money as it is needed, will pay for work, or will give an allowance because the children are "part of the family." There seems to be a common feeling that money is either shared or earned.

None of the parents in our study indicated that money for the children was a particularly difficult problem. Many did what seemed appropriate at the time, changing their strategy as the times, needs, and children changed. One couple wrote: "As with so many other areas, we have tried a lot of different things. One thing worked for one child and another for another. We don't see how some parents set up one system and hold to that as if it were the only way. If we had done that we couldn't have made allowances a helpful system in dealing with our children. Money is a tool, not the master; whom the money is given to is a tool, too, not a master.

103

Chapter Eight

THE HUSBAND-WIFE RELATIONSHIP

Although this study focused on parenting in effective families, it is impossible not to consider the effect of the husband-wife relationship on their ability to provide love and direction to the children. In the well-known words of President David O. McKay, "The best thing you can do for your children is to love their mother."

As we interviewed the less-effective families, several of them indicated problems in their marriage as well as dissatisfaction with their parenting. "We do not have what I would call a special family," said one woman sadly. "In almost every way we have botched it. Our family fights a lot, and the marriage has about come apart for a number of reasons. I doubt we could do any better if we were going to begin again with a fresh start. Nobody taught us to be parents, and I guess we didn't get it from instinct."

Another wife also expressed the same sense of near-hopelessness: "Finances have been tough for a long time, and we fight about it a lot. My husband works all the time and is never home much. Things aren't too happy for us."

One couple had actually divorced, then remarried. "We try harder, but it doesn't always work out," they said. The wife wrote that one of the best things they had going for them was their "strong determination to lead a fairly happy life in spite of major differences in husband and wife." Another woman admitted, "It's hard to get the children to understand that marriage is really important when I have been divorced two times."

104

For some, any kind of satisfaction in the marriage was almost completely gone. One woman observed flatly, "My husband hasn't told me that he loves me since we were married over twenty years ago." A husband admitted, "I just got some time on my hands and started seeing this other woman, and one thing led to another and everything just sort of fell apart."

No marriage is trouble free. The highly effective couples in our study are the last to claim any special exemption from problems. But they seem to have found out how to keep a high-quality, committed relationship as a husband and wife. As one wife said: "We are so pleased that we were raised when couples worked out their problems instead of giving up the marriage as so many now do. This is one thing that we have really talked about with our children. No marriage is perfect, but it becomes more so as problems are worked out with love and understanding. After all, this earth life is to build both here and for eternal worlds. Good families move right into the next life."

We asked each couple several questions about household chores, decisions, and general happiness:

1. In your present family, who usually does each of these tasks:

    Earns family income?
    Does the housekeeping?
    Keeps in touch with relatives?
    Organizes family recreation?
    Cares for preschool children?
    Teaches, helps, and disciplines girls ages 6-12?
    Teaches, helps, and disciplines boys ages 6-12?
    [We asked them to check one of five choices:
    husband entirely, husband more, both equally
    wife more, wife entirely.]

2. Who makes most of the decisions about: Earning family income?
    Doing the housekeeping?

105

Keeping in touch with relatives?
Family recreation?
Sexual intimacy?
Duties and behavior of girls ages 6-12?
Duties and behavior of boys ages 6-12?
[We asked them to mark one of the same five choices as above.]

3. All things considered, please indicate the degree of happiness of your marriage by marking an x on the following scale:

Very happy   9 8 7 6 5 4 3 2 1   Very unhappy
marriage   marriage

The parents in the sample responded this way:

Scale Number	Percent
3	2%
5	2%
6	2%
7	8%
8	16%
9	71%

The mean or average score for all of the families was 8.5, a very high perception of the happiness in their marriages. Nearly three-fourths of the parents felt their marriage was a 9. One Washington man and his second wife (his first had died) had been married for about eight years when they took this survey. The wife circled 9 and drew sunbeams around it, adding, "We feel that our marriage is very rewarding to us. We are best friends." One national survey with a similar scale showed 20 percent of the couples reporting "unhappy" marriages while the rest were "relatively happy." (Leslie Gerald, *The Family in Social Context* [New York: Oxford, 1979].) In a 1983 study of 200,000 people, 81 percent of the married respondents would marry their present spouse if they had it all to do over again, and 79 percent indicated that their "expectations of happiness are being fulfilled." (Better Homes and Gardens, *What's Happening to American Families?* [New York: Meredith Corporation, 1983].)

It's logical to suspect a certain bias in the response to this question since these parents knew they were a part of a study looking at good LDS families, and they may have felt some pressure to indicate they felt their marriage was a happy one. Still, 30 percent marked below the highest score, indicating some areas of disturbance, and 4 percent placed themselves at the midpoint or lower.

We can draw two inferences from these scores. On the one hand, it would seem that effective families are led by parents who have a very positive feeling about the happiness of their marriage. On the other hand, it seems possible in some cases to have a family that the stake president and others regard as highly effective even though the marriage is less than ideally happy. Very few people wrote comments about the marital score itself, but one wife commented that the financial worries were their chief problem, with sexual incompatibility next. Another wife indicated a lower happiness score than her husband and penciled in: "It's that darn money!"

None of the families we interviewed would say they have a perfect marriage, and all admitted to having real problems and adjustments as they have lived together. They have had personality differences. One spouse wanted to talk things out, the other didn't. Expectations about how to run a home or rear children have differed. But through it all the couples have had a common set of goals and values and a desire to stay together and be a happy family.

What are some patterns that contribute to harmony or to dissatisfaction? This table shows how the husband and wife in these families divided up certain tasks.

Task	Husband Entirely	Husband More	Equal	Wife Entirely	Wife More
Earns family income	62%	34%	3%	.5%	.5%
Housekeeping		1%	3%	70%	26%
Keeps in touch with relatives		3%	37%	54%	6%
Organizes family recreation		9%	58%	31%	2%
Cares for pre-school children			10%	77%	13%
Teaches, helps, and disciplines girls ages 6-12		3%	52%	44%	1%
Teaches, helps, and disciplines boys ages 6-12		8%	56%	35%	1%

As we look at these duties, the only one that was clearly the domain of the father was earning the family income, while the mother was clearly responsible for keeping up the house and taking care of the preschool children. This is a predictable pattern in couples of their generation and matches what we know of Americans in general from national data.

The mother's rather exclusive responsibility for preschoolers shifted once the children entered school. As the parents reported, more than 50 percent of the fathers worked with children of both sexes ages six to twelve.

Husbands sometimes took the responsibility for planning family recreation, although they were likely to share this task equally with their wives. One wife remarked wryly, "My husband plans a lot of his own recreation but not much for the whole family." However another husband, reflecting on the general topic of divisions of labor, wrote: "It takes a lot of effort to make money for the family to obtain the things my wife and I have decided are important. She doesn't work outside the home, but believe me, she works hard—I think much harder than I do. Her work is really never done. I try to help with the children and with things in the home all I can, but admittedly most if it falls to her. I love her for what she does, and someday perhaps I will be able to do more. It makes me feel bad when I see how some of the husbands I know try to get out of helping their wives by staying away or going on a lot of fishing trips. Women are pretty special to do so much and complain so little."

As the data on household chores revealed, most parents taught both sons and daughters to do most tasks, although boys were more commonly assigned to yard work, car repairs, working in the garden or the fields, and dealing with ranch animals, while girls were more likely to be assigned cooking, housecleaning, and doing dishes. It is expected that these same patterns would hold for mother and father. It would be interesting to see, in view of the national trends toward more egalitarian marriages, if this parental pattern is modified in their children's families.

After looking at the tasks, we then asked how decisions were made in the following areas:

Decision	Husband Entirely	Husband More	Equal	Wife Entirely	Wife More
Earns family income	28%	52%	21%		
Housekeeping		1%	7%	66%	26%
Keeps in touch with relatives		2%	52%	42%	4%
Family recreation		8%	75%	17%	1%
Sexual intimacy	2%	28%	65%	5%	
Duties of girls ages 6-12			52%	46%	1%
Duties of boys ages 6-12		18%	58%	23%	1%

Comparing responses, we see a general parallel between parents and children, but it is also clear that many couples make joint decisions even though only one will actually perform the task. For example, even though earning the family income is predominantly the husband's task, 21 percent of the wives said they have an equal voice in making decisions about their husband's work. One wife explained: "My husband and I talk over every decision he makes about his work. In the past we have jointly decided not to take a promotion that meant moving the family. We have resisted work assignments that interfered with Sunday activities or family vacations. I feel I should have a say in those kinds of work decisions that affect the family." One Utah couple, with the husband in his early fifties and the wife in her mid-forties, described a traditional relationship that seems to work in a very egalitarian way: "We have a patriarch in our home who loves the Lord and is committed to obeying his commandments, including teaching our four children. He is also willing to accept and implement suggestions from me. We work well as a family presidency and have regular meetings to plan for the family."

Several couples expressed strong feelings on the subject of marital unity. One Utah couple in their mid-forties with five children wrote that "husband-wife unity—a strong relationship through thick and thin!" was one of the most important factors in making them a strong family. Another Utah couple with nine children, ages seven to twenty-two reported: "We as marriage partners are in love and are absolutely committed to each other. As parents we are absolutely committed to the gospel. We work hard at teaching our children what is right and at helping to channel them, but we respect their free agency." One Washington wife wrote: "We feel that because we, as husband and wife, have a great feeling of love and respect for one another and a very rewarding relationship, that this will set an example for our children and help them to have happy marriages. Our one married child has a happy marriage."

A Utah couple with nine children ranging from nine to twenty-four observed, "We feel a sense of security in the concept 'Love is harmony even in discord.'" An Idaho couple strongly believed in "sticking together on discipline, whether they agreed at the time or not."

In another Utah family, also perceived as highly effective, the parents acknowledged strong differences between them. The husband commented, "Our compatibility has grown somewhat less as my wife's education has increased. However, we have tried to keep our differences from our seven children." They had marked two places on the marital happiness scale, the wife about an 8 and the husband about a 7. At other points in the survey they had written their own answers when they differed from each other. For instance, the husband felt that the most important factor in the family's success was "going to church together," while the wife felt that it was "letting our children know—no matter what—that we really love them." The husband had felt that the children "must do" all of the activities they had checked, while the wife "doesn't like the term 'must.'" They had also rated their preferred discipline styles differently from each other. Obviously, they were able to acknowledge and deal with these differences, not feeling that differences paralyzed the marriage or had to be concealed.

We added the issue of the couple's sexual intimacy since this is a much-studied area nationally. With sixty-five percent of these couples, decisions about intimacy seemed to be shared. In 28 percent of the cases, the husband was seen as more influential in these decisions. (Nationally, 80 percent of both spouses indicated that sexual activity is initiated by the husband. [F. Ivan Nye, *Role Structure and Analysis of the Family* (Beverly Hills, Calif.: Sage Publications), p. 105.] Two percent indicated that the husband was completely responsible for decisions about intimacy. We do not have data to determine if this is acceptable to the wife or whether it is a point of disturbance in the relationship. Our data also show that in 5 percent of the cases, decisions about intimacy are primarily the responsibility of the wife. Again our data do not show if the wife's decision is to initiate or resist intimacy.)

As we would expect from couples of this generation, they considered sexual intimacy to be a personal and private matter, not one to be discussed openly. Respecting these feelings, we did not probe deeply during the follow-up interviews. One couple shared this appraisal: "We have found that our sex life has undergone a lot of changes through the years. Early in our marriage there was concern about pregnancies, and we never completely resolved our feelings about using birth control methods. There was often a difference in the eagerness and energy we had toward responding to each other. The wife was often tired from a lot of work with a lot of children and outside assignments. It seemed that for a time she would go along to meet the needs of the husband. As children have gone from the home and we have fewer pressures, our own relationship has become more important and more satisfying, although there is still some imbalance in terms of who has the stronger needs."

Sexual incompatibility is often cited by nonprofessionals as a "cause" of divorce, but statistics show very little correlation between marital happiness and sexual satisfaction. (Randall Collins, *Sociology of Marriage and the Family* [Chicago: Prentice-Hall, 1985], p. 249.) However, it is probably true that sexual problems are symptomatic of other problems. Couples who are angry over money problems or exhausted by fights with their teenagers may use the sexual relationship as a weapon in fighting about their differences.

Probably many of the couples in the survey would agree with one couple's analysis of their own compatibility: "Our answers to these questions as to how happy our marriage is and how various decisions are made will vary depending on such things as stress, pressures, mood, cycles, and health." Other families have indicated that while they have a generally consistent pattern of making decisions, shifts and variations in circumstances will cause "periodic readjustments and fluctuations."

A Utah couple in their mid-sixties with seven children wrote, "Our family has been our top priority. As parents we have desired some individuality too, not just living for our children. We have felt that the things we pursued together as a family have been important—additional education, cultural refinement, missions, building homes together, civic and church involvement. All of these things have enhanced our children's involvement."

For another couple, the key to successful parenting is that "there was always unity between husband and wife. We shared Church positions, welfare assignments, and meetings. Our children also shared in all of these things because it was part of family life." A Wyoming couple in their early fifties, the youngest of their six children now eighteen, agreed that the most important factor in making a strong family was "acting together as husband and wife, as mother and father, and always keeping a strong front."

The high commitment to gospel ideals and the deliberate, long-term cultivation of love in the home that nearly all of these effective couples have achieved are both signs that the husband and wife closely shared the same interests and goals. It is a truism that couples with similar goals and values have happier, less stressful marriages. Many years ago, a popular notion was that "opposites attract" and that differences made the marriage more interesting. However, enough inevitable differences exist in most marriages that it is unneccessary to advise a couple to look for more. One couple wrote: "We used to have more problems in our marriage than we do now. We never really had too many serious problems, just the little things that come along now and again. Well, they don't come along so much anymore, and we would say that we have never been happier in our marriage. We started out happy, and things have really just gotten better all the time. We thought we were happy then, but we are happier now. We have always thought that we couldn't be happier, but each year gets better, especially as the children have gotten older."

These effective couples have highly compatible values. They want the same things for their children—missions, temple marriage, education, strong family ties. They have been willing to spend their time and money on the family.

They have generally had large families and devoted a great deal of time to teaching them, encouraging them, and modeling Church teachings for them. They have spent a lot of time talking with and teaching their children.

It has been their goal to rear a good family, to prepare as much as they could to be a family that might be a candidate for a celestial heritage. All of these families acknowledged certain weaknesses and shortcomings. But the essence of their lives is clearly that they have tried to live as close to the standards and values they believe in as they can. They want to be a close, unified family. One couple wrote: "We fell in love a long time ago and made the commitment to team up in this life. Some of the time we had difficulties, but we have worked at it, and we think we love each other more as the years go by. Some of the hardest times were when most of the children were starting to get older, but we stuck it out. We really do love each other, and our children sense that. We talk and share. We pray together and do a lot of planning about our family. We think the Lord helps us a lot in our marriage and with our kids."

An almost mirror reversal of this position is the statement of the husband in one of the less-effective families: "We have had our share of problems as a family. My wife and I have not been able to get along like we should always. Some of our kids have 'acted out,' at times and this has brought us a lot of embarrassment and so on. I see a lot of families who seem to have things together, and how I wish we could be more like them. I don't know, I guess we made our bed and now we have to sleep in it. All of my sisters' families do well, and my wife's brothers and sisters do well too, but we just have had a hard time. I guess we love each other, but most of the time it doesn't get demonstrated very well."

Which comes first—a good marriage or good parenting? It's probably impossible ever to decide. But when parents are truly committed to family-centered goals, they seem happy together in their marriages and feel that what they are accomplishing is good. The sense of contentment they feel is real.

Chapter Nine

ADVERSITY: COPING
WITH DIFFICULT
TIMES

We wanted to know how much of the effectiveness of the families we surveyed came from good circumstances ("we raised our children on a ranch away from many temptations and distractions") and how much depended on the character and decisions of the parents. We asked each couple four questions:

1. Has your family ever encountered any real family problems or adversities?
2. If so, what were they?
3. How long did they last?
4. How did you handle them?

We wanted to probe what constituted adversity for these families and what their coping mechanisms were. The evidence seems to be that even though the families had experienced difficulties, they were able to cope with them; and as many families indicated, the problems have strengthened them.

When we asked, "Have you experienced any real family problems or adversities?" about 20 percent answered "no." Another 30 percent said they had experienced several severe problems, and the other 50 were in between—they had had some real problems, but not what they considered to be an unusual number.

These percentages are probably on the low side. During our follow-up interviews, we found that some couples who had marked "no real problems" had in fact faced a number of problems including long-term unemployment, illnesses, and disappointments with children. However, they compared themselves to others who had suffered the death of a child or permanent disability of a family member and felt that their problems were relatively insignificant. One couple told us: "We have had problems, but we just never thought of them as special problems. If illness, death, and financial problems are problems, we have had them, but Job suffered more, and we think that one purpose of this life is to encounter problems, so we certainly wouldn't single ourselves out as anything special on this account. It's true that many whom we know seem to have clearer sailing in this life. Perhaps the Lord will test them in some other manner."

Another husband offered an explanation: "We have had a number of family problems in our married life. I have had a heart attack, but recovered. We have had to take care of aged parents for many years. My wife's brothers and sisters have had divorces and problems. But in our own family we have been blessed. Our boys have all filled missions. Our daughter married a fine young man in the temple. Compared to other families we know, we really have never had any real problems."

Among the families who were willing to define their problems as adversities, these difficulties appeared:

1. Health problems
   (illness, disabilities, accidents)   40%
2. A rebellious or problem child   19%
3. Death of family member(s)   15%
4. Business or financial reversals   14%
5. Word of Wisdom problems
   (drugs, alcohol, etc.)   4%
6. Divorce   3%
7. Fire or other natural disasters   3%

National measures of family stress usually turn up the same problems: divorce, death, drugs, alcohol, abuse, unemployment, and so on. The families in our survey clearly define health problems as the major difficulty they have had to face. It is interesting that to some extent illness and accidents are outside the control of individuals (that is, people do not "decide" to be sick or healthy), while the second greatest problem, a rebellious child, is a matter of someone's will (that is, the child decides to depart from the family norms and values).

These good families are not problem free. They have drunk from the bitter cup. But they also seem to have been able to cope with these problems instead of being devastated by them. When we asked how long they had suffered from these adversities, 63 percent responded that they had faced the situations for years, and another 24 percent indicated the problems had lasted for many months. Several people who had suffered deaths in the family wrote comments like "When is a death 'over'?" These problems, in other words, are not short-term matters.

In response to the question about how they had handled their adversity, about 35 percent of the couples said that they had turned to the Lord in prayer, fasting, and exercising their faith. About an equal number (30 percent) described a process of accepting the situation, developing patience, and assuming the burden of living successfully with the adverse condition. ("We lived through it," is a stoical comment that appeared more than once.)

Another group (22 percent) said that the family had pulled together and strengthened each other so they could deal with the situation, whether it involved a solution to the problem or developing the patience to live with it. One Texas couple with six children had suffered illnesses, the death of loved ones, and financial difficulties. "We handled them one day at a time," they explained. "Fasting, prayer, and the support of each other all helped."

More than seventy-five of the 200 families explained their problems in enough detail that we could glimpse both their dimensions and their solutions.

In one Utah family with nine children, the husband

was disabled and ill during most of the years the children were growing up. For a good many years, he was confined to a wheelchair and threatened with the loss of his legs. His inability to work and provide for his family was a secondary but very real problem. His wife wrote, "We try to make our problems pay off for us by being thankful for our added time together and looking at the positive side of problems." Among those positive aspects were the children's learning to rely on the Spirit and the unity fostered by working for the common good. The children have also always contributed their income to a common fund.

A Texas couple with four children had endured illnesses and broken bones among the children and the much more disruptive illnesses of the parents—open-heart surgery for the father, thyroid surgery for the mother. "Self-reliance and keeping an eternal perspective have helped," they wrote. "Prayers are important and very strengthening to all of us."

A Utah couple recalled as their greatest times of trouble a terrifying two-week crisis when they almost lost one of their eight children to spinal meningitis and a longer crisis when their eldest daughter ran away at age sixteen. "That crisis lasted six months—maybe it isn't completely over yet," wrote the mother. They had dealt with the first crisis by "lots of prayer and communicating" for emotional support and used the same method in trying to reach their daughter again. "Professional counseling also helped," she added.

With "faith in the gospel and much prayer, we made it through," wrote a Montana farm couple with five living children. A sixth had died and another had Down's syndrome; drought and hail had decimated their crops; and various accidents around the farm had been debilitating to other members of the family.

A Utah couple with eight children had one child who required open-heart surgery, brain surgery, and numerous hospital stays. Another child involved in a car accident was hospitalized for a long time and required eye surgery, physical therapy, occupational therapy, and special schools. The family finances suffered, and the mother fought recurring bouts of depression. "We handled it by dropping everything else and just carrying on," wrote the father.

A young daughter in one family developed cystic fibrosis. "Everyone knew that this was a terminal disease," reported the father. "All of the other children, both older and younger, treated this little girl with special care. She was a beautiful, loving child anyway. You couldn't help but love her. But she was the one that everyone tried to help, be with, or do for."

One Idaho farmer, now seventy-eight, lost his first wife when she died at age thirty-one, leaving five living children. Their first child had died. His second wife bore eight children in ten years and died at age thirty-four. A third marriage, which produced five surviving children and two babies who died soon after birth, again ended with the death of his wife at age fifty. His fourth wife brought eight children to the marriage. He also laconically listed "several serious accidents, crop failures, etc." among his moments of adversity, commenting that "they lasted from one to the next." In answer to the question about how he handled them, his wife wrote: "1 Nephi 3:7." That scripture says, "I will go and do the things which the Lord hath commanded, for I know that the Lord giveth no commandments unto the children of men, save he shall prepare a way for them that they may accomplish the thing which he commandeth them."

For twenty of their almost-thirty-year marriage, one Idaho couple coped with their particular adversity: their second child of six was killed at the age of ten in a sleighing accident. Her younger brother became handicapped, couldn't walk, and died at the age of nineteen. All four grandparents died. "Being close together is the way we gained strength," they wrote.

A Wyoming couple with five children stoically listed "death of a baby, home fire, cancer and the loss of Mother's leg, health and surgery, and taking over the family ranch" among their adversities, handled by "prayer, fasting, and blessings, and a lot of family communication."

One Washington family underwent the strain of losing their mother to death when the four children were between the ages of five and twelve. The second marriage added two children to the family and readjustments to all, over the succeeding fifteen years. "One boy acted out a great deal of anger," the parents wrote, "but loves his family. A healing still needs to take place with all the older children in regard to their mother's death. They all have some anger and will not attend church now; however, they are very responsible and independent people. The grief gets better with time, but it will never end. There is always an empty spot for Mom. It's a challenge to build and maintain unity; but we love the gospel and our children. We've experienced times when only our faith in God gave us hope and encouragement. We have seen miracles take place in seemingly simple ways and feel that we have great blessings."

One Texas couple with five children suffered deeply when their oldest daughter went through three or four years of flouting family standards and finally gave birth to a child out of wedlock. "We try to be there when she needs us," they explained, "but we want her to be responsible. We backed off on giving advice and we also backed off on giving help. We have not helped financially with the baby."

One Utah managment consultant had to work abroad for a year, a time that his wife acknowledged as a strain. All of their seven children who were old enough graduated from seminary; the boys who were old enough served missions; but one daughter did not marry in the temple. The wife felt that dealing with this "child who wouldn't follow counsel" had been a source of adversity that they had handled "with much prayer and fasting, and relying on the Spirit. On occasion," she added, "we have sought counsel from professionals in the problem area—usually someone we knew already who advised us about specific problems."

A Texas couple with five children recalled concern over the poor grades of one child and the troubled marriage of an older daughter. "In both cases," they wrote, "we got professional evaluation and counseling, and we gave our personal advice and support."

A Montana couple with six children were grieved when three of the six had "morality problems," but the problems did not last long and all three went to the bishop on their own.

A Texas couple with five children were saddened by the long-term inactivity of their oldest child ("He has since returned"). They describe themselves as "a very affectionate family. We love each other and tell it often." Thus, it was an area of special pain when their oldest daughter's in-laws misunderstood her, creating a problem that lasted about two years. "Fasting, prayer, and love is how we handled both problems," wrote the mother.

A Montana couple with seven children had one son who "found himself in serious trouble with the authorities." During the three-month ordeal, they tried to keep their problem in perspective: "Every family has its share of crummy happenings. You handle them with prayer, love, and support for whoever needs it." The lesson they learned was "bending with the adversity so as not to break," but still, they confessed, "it's awfully hard, putting away wonderful beautiful dreams about a child's life and just standing behind him, loving him no matter what."

A California couple with four children suffered the loss of their third child, which "brought the family even closer," they wrote. "We all want to be worthy to be with her again." Another problem was that the parents had a strong preference about which college one daughter should go to. They reported candidly, "She obeyed her father but hated it, so we let her go to her choice and it worked out fine. She was right, and we admitted it." Another couple, grieved when their son came home from his mission early, found the family, all ten children, "pulling more together and relying on the Lord." The son in one Idaho family accepted a mission call, then eloped. A daughter was diagnosed as having cancer, and the father nearly died from health problems that resulted in twenty days of hospitalization and six months of recuperation. "Prayer and family councils were our mainstay," wrote the mother.

In another Utah family with three children where a classic but hardly reassuring pattern of teenage rebellion, drug abuse, and dishonesty occurred, the parents handled it, "first with confrontation, then more with patience, prayer, and understanding." An Idaho couple with five children had a problem for about a year with one teenager's "improper reading materials, Word of Wisdom temptations, and spending habits." They handled the situation by "expressing our disappointment and explaining the hazards, then demonstrating increased love."

A Utah couple with five children struggled for twelve years with their rebellious eldest son who dropped out of school, stole, and was abusive to the other children. They worked with a counselor and their bishop, and resorted to foster placement for a month. They have seen him gradually return to Church activity, family relationships, and school. One couple with six children are still living in a nightmare that followed their eighteen-year-old son's report of homosexual rape. "We thought he was okay—just scared," they wrote. "Now he says he's homosexual, has rejected all authority, and has turned to homosexual friends." Two other couples mentioned the rape of a daughter.

Several parents mentioned, as a source of adversity, the negative influence of friends. A Utah couple with eight living children had undergone a two-year period of seeing their children influenced adversely by friends. Their method of dealing with the problem was "logic and encouraging new friends." One Montana couple with four children saw their eldest daughter begin dating nonmembers and, after six months, marry one. Another Montana couple had one daughter marry out of the temple and later divorce, as did a sister who had been married in the temple, who also suffered from experiments with drinking and smoking. In answer to the question "How did you handle these adversities?" the parents wrote from the heart, "We feel really bad."

One Texas family had taken care of a senile grandmother during the last three years of her life by "working together and talking a lot."

In one Utah family, the couple had married in the temple when they were both twenty-one or twenty-two. The husband is a university professor, and his long schooling had been a financial struggle for them, particularly since the first three of their five children were born within the next five years and the wife had had difficult pregnancies. They had faced their problems with "work, prayer, fasting, faith, and endurance."

One Utah couple with eight children had weathered a ten-year financial crisis coupled with the serious four-year illness of one family member by "pooling all our resources, including our talents, to deal with it." Adversity had made them "more considerate, helpful, and prayerful," they wrote. A Utah couple with seven children identified as a chief problem the financial difficulties caused by the husband's unsatisfactory employment. (He is currently a janitor.) "We endured job changes again and again for twenty-three years," the wife wrote. They rated their marital happiness at about an 8, and the wife jotted down: "Financial worries are the main problem" followed by sexual differences. (They had checked that decisions about sexual intimacy were equally shared.)

For another couple, adversities included the financial difficulties of a son who struggled to pay school debts and support his family. Although this couple has given and loaned money, along with providing occasional child care, advice, and blessings to all their married children, they comment, "Our son is still having money problems, but he's working them out. We helped some but feel he should handle it himself."

A Salt Lake City couple suffered severe financial reverses when the husband's partners embezzled from the firm. "Prayer, hard work, and being positive about the future" were chief strategies for handling these problems. An Idaho farm equipment manager with ten children found himself in serious financial difficulty when his partner pulled out, leaving them with all the debts to pay. He and his wife negotiated with the debtors and, over a five-year period, "paid off the obligations and cleared our name." Another Idaho couple discovered, when the husband was forty-eight, that their financial future had changed when the bank foreclosed on their business and the husband had to find a new occupation. They had already weathered the wife's three-year-long disability and managed, they felt, "very well."

An Idaho couple felt that their most serious problem was gradually being forced to realize that they could not make a living farming, especially when the third of their eight children was injured and permanently handicapped. After a three-year struggle, they sold the farm and went back to school, and both became teachers.

An Idaho family survived the year-long recuperation of a child scalded so badly that hospitalization was required for two months; but it took them three years to get back on their feet when their home was destroyed in the 1976 Teton Dam flood in southeastern Idaho. During both traumatic periods, they relied on "blessings, the psychological support of friends and family, keeping busy with hard work, and planning ahead even when there seemed to be no future."

Other types of problems also showed up on the questionnaire. One Utah couple with seven children had had a baby die, but the adversity they listed was overcome by "getting along, considering one another's feelings, overcoming selfishness and impatience." A Utah couple with four children experienced as their greatest trial one period when the husband had to work out of state for extended periods of time. "Thank goodness that only lasted a few months," wrote the wife, "and we got through with lots of prayer and fasting and our patriarchal blessings." One Texas couple mentioned marital problems as adversity, but added that "prayer, work, and faith had resolved them after a few weeks."

Only two couples said they had handled their problems "well" and conversely, only two or three said they had handled them "not too well." Thus, most of the families felt that they *had* handled their difficulties. To a remarkable degree, they also seemed to have handled them as internal problems and with internal resources. It is interesting that with all of the problems with health, not more than half a dozen families mentioned doctors as helping them cope with their problems, even though their technical assistance goes without saying. Approximately a dozen mentioned counselors or therapists as helping with the emotional problems, about the same number as those who mentioned bishops or other Church authorities. No doubt, as in the case of medical assistance, it goes without saying that some consulted professional people and their bishops, but apparently the coping process inside the family was not noticeably influenced by these professionals. Prayer, blessings, and fasting were often mentioned. The *Better Homes & Gardens* survey had asked couples to identify whom they turned to for help in confronting significant problems. Seventy-one percent reported that they turned to the family, 21 percent to friends, 10 percent to clergy, 7 percent to another member of their church, 2 percent to a co-worker, and 7 percent to "other." Thus, the family-centeredness of the effective families in our survey is emphasized by the comparison.

It is probably impossible to determine which came first—strength to handle adversity well or the adversity that produced increased strength. Certainly, working through their problems made these families stronger, no matter what the comparative strengths with which they began; and the feeling of success in coping with their problems would no doubt have increased their ability to deal with other forms of stress.

One couple quoted Ether 12:27 in an interview: "If men come unto me I will show unto them their weakness. I give unto men weakness that they may be humble; and my grace is sufficient for all men that humble themselves before me; for if they humble themselves before me, and have faith in me, then will I make weak things become strong unto them." They commented, "We think this is how working out problems happens in our family. For us, this scripture explains how the Lord uses problems to help people make something out of life."

Chapter Ten

FRIENDS AND DATES, SIBLINGS AND HEROES

Even though effective families, like effective corporations, seem to have strong internal "cultures," rules, norms, expectations, myths, and patterns of behavior, no family exists in a vacuum. We asked some questions to get some insight into how friends and older siblings influenced children, and we wondered if heroes outside the family had much impact. The questions were:

1. Please indicate for your children how many friends they had compared with most other children their age. (We then had a grid with the numbers of the children and the choices of "more friends," "the same number," and "fewer friends.")

2. Our children's friends
   ____ have been a very helpful influence for our children
   ____ have seldom been of value in our children's lives
   ____ have frequently led our children astray

3. When your children are with their friends, do they spend the time
   ____ mostly in the homes of the friends
   ____ about equally in each home
   ____ mostly in your home

4. Do you approve of your children's friends
   ____most of the time
   ____sometimes
   ____almost never
5. How important do you think your older
   children are in shaping the younger children?
   ____very important
   ____somewhat important
   ____not too important
   ____not at all important
6. If your older children help shape the younger
   ones, how do they do this? (We offered the
   choices of example, helping with school lessons,
   encouraging the younger ones to study or work
   hard, preparing talks, writing encouraging
   letters, attending functions where the young
   ones are participating, and "other.")
7. Do you have any heroes as a family? If so, who
   are they?

FRIENDS

Eighty-five percent of the families in the survey indicated that the children's friends have been a "very helpful"
influence. One couple checked that answer on their questionnaire but also reported that one daughter had married a
good but inactive man while another daughter's first marriage, which ended in divorce, had not been a temple marriage.

The number of friends seemed to be related to age.
Only 22 percent of first-born children had more friends
than most children their age, while about 33 percent of
most of the other children in the family had "more than
most." Furthermore, between 15 and 20 percent of the
families felt that their children as a whole had fewer friends
than most. In some cases, this perception may have simply
reflected the fact that there were plenty of children at home
to play with and that the family's emphasis on unity would
tend to draw children and their friends into the family,

rather than encouraging the children to seek companionship elsewhere.

A few parents expressed concern that a particular child did not have more friends. One couple wrote: "We always worried about our third child. He seemed to have a hard time making friends and always spent a lot of time doing things alone. We tried to invite children in and foster friendships, but it never was easy. Our other children all seemed to make friends easily and had lots of companions. It was hard for us to see this child left out when others were going places with their friends." However, another couple said, "Our youngest son didn't have very many friends, but he did have one or two with whom he was very close. This seemed to satisfy his friendship needs, so we didn't worry too much because these close friends were good boys and had a good influence on him." A Texas couple with seven children took the long view in pointing out that their second son had had only one friend all through high school; "but now that he's in college he has many and is more open and lively."

Thirteen percent of the parents felt that some of their children's friends had "seldom" been a positive influence, and 2 percent felt that some of these friends had been downright negative in leading them away from family norms. One Utah couple with five children checked the "very helpful" box but wrote, "Friends led one child astray temporarily." A second Utah couple with six children also checked the "very helpful" box but qualified their answer: "One child had problems for a period of time with friends we would not have chosen." An Idaho couple wrote that friends have "sometimes" been of value in their children's lives, explaining, "There are some exceptions; but generally they have had to learn to stand up for their own convictions."

One father denied any significant impact from friends by observing, "Our children's friends have been of great value to them but have not influenced their basic values— either for good or for bad." One Montana couple who checked "seldom" observed, "We live in a very small branch, and most of the children's friends have been non-members."

Still, it seems clear that the friends of the children generally had an important positive influence on them and 95 percent of the parents said they had approved of their children's friends most of the time.

Among the 5 percent who registered a negative vote was a mother who told us in an interview, "Our children played with the most active families in our ward, but we found sometimes their influence was against observance of Church standards (for example, observing the Sabbath, no R-rated movies, no dating until sixteen). This resulted in a situation where we seemed to be the only family pushing for the observance of church counsel."

One couple reported: "We had a lot of trouble with one daughter because of the friends she had. They had different values, and she was always in some sort of difficulty with them. As we talked about it, we decided to intervene more directly and encouraged her to have parties in our home to which she invited other girls. She sort of discovered that it was fun to have other friends—friends who reinforced family values rather than presenting her with conflicts."

When we asked parents whether children generally brought their friends to their home or went to their friends' homes, 34 percent answered "mostly in our home," 57 percent found the time divided about equally between friends' homes and their own home, and only 8 percent indicated that their children spent most of their time in the homes of their friends. The Utah mother of nine explained a family policy of discouraging the children from spending "a lot of time with friends outside of the family" (there is an absolute prohibition on sleep-overs) but noted that "our younger children possibly play more elsewhere than the older ones did because they don't have as many brothers and sisters at home." A Utah couple with six living children observed that the children mostly brought their friends home, except for one boy who "loves to be everywhere. Everyone is his family." One mother of six, during an interview, reflected mixed feelings about having her home as the neighborhood hang-out: "I was usually glad that our children's friends wanted to come to our home. It was fun to have lots of kids in the house—parties, music, talking. But I have to admit that sometimes I would wish that just some of the time they would go to somebody else's house besides ours. I would have liked to see some of the other mothers prepare the food or snacks and then clean up after everyone had gone home."

DATES

We did not ask specific questions about the children's dating patterns and partners; but as we expected, a number of parents mentioned them. If they mentioned dating ages, it was usually to stress their insistence that the children wait until age sixteen to begin dating. Twenty-three percent of the parents identified peer influence and attractive influences outside the home as the factors that made it hardest to raise teenagers.

One Utah couple expressed real ambiguity about their youngest daughter's insistence on dating only Latinos. An elder sister had already undergone a divorce, and they were concerned about potential instability in another marriage. "We are trying to handle this situation with love, support, and nonjudgmental attitudes," they wrote. "They have all been fine young men, and we've included them in our family activities; but by so doing, we are in fact okaying the relationship. This is a conflict for us." A California couple with three children was dismayed when their only daughter insisted on going steady through most of her high-school years against their wishes. They tried to handle the situation with "patience and love" rather than direct confrontation.

A Wyoming couple with seven children recalls "dating controversies" as a major form of adversity, which they tried to handle with "love and concern." An Idaho couple,

131

also with seven children, considered a long-term relationship of one daughter's a major difficulty in their life. "They were going steady in high school and wanted to marry. We didn't want them to," they wrote. The parents' way of dealing with the situation was "patience and talking with the boy. He spent so much time here he felt like our son." The problem was resolved as the two teenagers "became very bored with each other and broke up, and our daughter went to college."

One couple felt that a beneficial rule for their teenagers had been that they could not own a motorized vehicle until after they left home. Although the children with licenses had generous access to the family car, this rule meant that parents continued to exercise a good deal of supervision over their whereabouts. Another couple held out firmly against the local popularity of dirt-bikes and motorcycles for the same reason. Other parents had driving-related rules: no driving until after driver's education; no driving for sons until they had become Eagle Scouts; no driving if the grades slipped below a certain level; no driving without permission. Family members who drove had to help transport others. One couple wrote: "We found it was a great help in the family when the older children learned to drive. Then they could take the younger ones to school, Church functions, seminary, ball games, and so on."

Since dating, courtship, and establishing independent families represent a crucial "launching" period for young people, it would be interesting to know how much parents did before dating age to help their children internalize Church and family rules, how much local customs from area to area of the United States were allowed to influence their children, and what synthesis the children made for themselves.

SIBLING INFLUENCE

We did not ask parents to compare the influence of friends with the influence of brothers and sisters, but we suspect that siblings would rate much higher than friends.

Eight-eight percent of the couples responded that their elder children were "very important" in training the younger children. Another 11 percent felt that they were "somewhat" important. Not a single couple checked "not at all important." One father, who had been raised in a family of twelve children, recalled that his own father had often said, "Mother and I reared the first six and then they reared the last six." He and his wife felt that their own children had followed much the same pattern.

This is how parents rated the influence of the elder children:

1.	Being an example	97%
2.	Attending functions when younger ones are participating	92%
3.	Encouraging younger ones to study or work hard	80%
4.	Helping with school work	75%
5.	Writing letters of encouragement	57%
6.	Helping prepare talks	40%
7.	Playing with them and being a friend	40%

Written-in comments on the "other" line included "sharing books they've enjoyed," "including young ones in many of their activities," "encouragement in Scouting, physical fitness, grooming, and manners," teaching them dancing, piano, and songs," "passing their jobs from one to another and expecting them to do as well," "training them in sports," "helping them reason out problem situations," "helping them see the importance of the family and doing well," "playing together a lot, particularly in areas where the parents don't share the same interests," "playing ball with them," "being interested in each other's welfare," "being a good friend," and "participating in family activities even after they are married."

Many parents had commented in one place or another that they consistently counted on the older children to tend the younger ones in the absence of the parents.

133

Several parents added comments about the influence of their children on each other. One mother remarked, "I don't know how we would have reared the younger children in the family without the great example of our eldest child. She had such a sweet, loving disposition and was always so helpful that all of the other children loved her and wanted to be like her. She made it easy for us to keep all the rest on the right path." The California mother of four observed that one of the most effective forms of discipline in their family was "pressure from other siblings to do what was right."

An Idaho couple with seven children discovered that the nature of discipline in their family had changed as the children grew older because the three older children actually did a great deal of parenting for the younger four. With a touch of humor, the mother wrote: "I asked our three older children how many rules we have, and they said, 'Oh, *lots!* When we were little anyway. Now there don't seem to be *any* for the younger four brothers and sisters.'

"I asked the younger ones and they answered, 'Oh, *lots!*'

"'What are some?'

"'Oh, I guess to obey is the only one.'

"The older children feel that their father and I have really become less strict through the years—perhaps with some foundation in fact, although if we did, it was unintentional. The younger children have the older children and their friends for examples as well as us. Many times as parents we've found ourselves taking sides with a younger child who has violated a rule; but when three or four siblings pounce on them for correction, the parents don't also need to pounce."

The Utah father of five closely spaced children recalled, "We soon discovered that we relied heavily on our eldest, a boy, to set the example and be responsible for the others. Like many other parents, we saw (too late to change much) that what we expected was a quantum leap more demanding than what we expected from the youngest. But the elder ones did look after the younger ones. They always went to the others' ball games or programs. They set the pattern for Church attendance, good grades, mission preparation, and general obedience."

Another father wrote, "I will always be grateful for the great example our eldest daughter set for the rest of the children. She had such a great spirit—never complained, pouted, or rebelled. We could count on her to get behind the things we were trying to accomplish. She worked hard in school, got good grades, and had a sensitive feeling for spiritual things. All of this rubbed off on the younger ones."

Only two couples indicated that older children could sometimes be negative examples. "In our family the older ones are so involved in themselves they don't always have time for anyone outside themselves," wrote one mother. A Texas couple with five children wrote, "Our older children were not always a good example, so the younger ones knew what they should *not* do." One girl remarked, "I learned from the tough experiences my older brother had with our parents. He would get into trouble with the folks and I would learn what not to do."

HEROES

We asked about family heroes in an effort to determine whether parents deliberately selected people worthy of emulation and held them up as models for their children. In retrospect, we wished that we had specifically asked about "heroes and heroines," since almost no one identified women as role models. Our phrasing may have influenced parents to think only of men in their answers.

Also, by asking the parents, we excluded many individual models. It is possible that a whole different set of names would emerge if we had asked the children to identify their own heroes instead of asking the parents to identify family heroes. In fact, a few questionnaires specified "no family heroes" but listed people who were heroes for certain individuals or groups in the family. For instance, in one California family with four children, the twenty-one-year-old son had President Ronald Reagan as a hero, the twenty-year-old daughter had Marie Osmond, and the husband had Bob Hope.

Still, the results are interesting. Forty-nine percent either said they had no family heroes or qualified the question in some way. For example, one Idaho couple wrote, "There are many people we admire but no heroes." Another Idaho couple observed, "We respect our Church leaders, especially our bishop, but we don't have heroes." One couple identified *M*A*S*H* as a family hero but did not specify which characters in the show they particularly enjoyed. A Montana couple with eight children identified as family heroes "those who are righteously successful," while a Salt Lake City couple with five children said their family heroes were "stong, active, loving, friendly men in our ward."

When we analyzed who the listed heroes were—either as first or second choices—we got these results:

President Spencer W. Kimball	51%
Church leaders (as a group)	46%
Other relatives	44%
Parents	42%
Sports figures	24%
Political leaders	18%
Jesus Christ	8%
Movie stars	8%

We found it interesting that family members are mentioned as heroes less often than President Kimball but more often than LDS athletes like Johnny Miller, Steve Young, or Danny Ainge.

One couple, who identified some as ancestors as family heroes, explained: "We have had some fine grandparents who are really special to us. They were among the early converts to the Church, and they did a lot for our family in setting a good example. Their lives were not easy. Some of their little children were buried along the way West. They built a new home in a new area without assistance from anyone but the Lord. We don't need any hero from out in the world somewhere. We have great heroes in our own family."

In a family of four, the mother consulted the children on the question of heroes. "Our daughter said, 'Hannah Dustin!' She is an ancestor who was captured by Indians, scalped a great number of them, and helped two others captured with her to escape. We visited her monument one year on vacation when our daughter was about eleven. Her brother, who was six at the time of this vacation, also mentioned Hannah. Other heroes are Spencer W. Kimball and John W. Hess, another ancestor."

A Montana couple with seven children wrote: "Husband likes LeGrand Richards. We all agree on Jesus Christ, Nephi, Joseph Smith, Moroni, President Kimball, and John Glenn. I'm sorry it's such a sarcastic world. It's hard to find someone contemporary to emulate." A Utah family for whom culture was important listed "great artists, authors, and musicians" among their heroes. An Idaho family with seven children observed, "We all follow BYU sports, but the children look up to their grandparents more than anyone we know. They were strong, exceptional people. Even the older married children talk of them and their ideals." A Utah couple wrote, "Jesus Christ is always mentioned as our model, yet to call him a hero is somewhat sacrilegious!" A Utah family with seven children listed Walt Disney, Nephi, and "pilots."

Another family had a long list: "Jesus Christ, President Kimball, a German soccer player, Kane in the TV series 'Kung Fu,' Patriarch Copeland, the family in 'The Little House on the Prairie,' Danny White, and Merlin Olsen."

CONCLUSION

Effective families do not exist in a vacuum. But they do seem to pay a great deal of attention to the values held by those who associate with their children, and they train their older children carefully. The payoff is that these older children almost always perpetuate the parents' values in dealing with the younger children so that the family can have a strong internal culture, a clear sense of "this is how we do things in our family." Friends have a generally positive influence on the children, probably because the children unconsciously select friends with similar values for the most part, and partly because the family culture also affects these friends. The fact that almost 85 percent of family heroes are either other family members, Church authorities, or other Church members only reinforces the already strong pattern of family values.

Chapter Eleven

FAMILY GOALS

Effective families can tell if they're making progress because they know where they're going. These parents articulate a clear vision of what they want for the whole family and for each family member—"Being together forever." Planning on forever, they are strongly motivated to maintain a high degree of unity and affection within the family. When inevitable adversities come, it is toward each other that they turn for support.

We asked parents, "What special goals do you have as a family?" We offered some choices, and here's how they responded:

Have children go on missions	100%
Have children marry in the temple	100%
Have children get good educations	99%
Develop a strong sense of family unity	98%
Help each child to develop a strong feeling of self-worth or a good self-concept	97%
Have everyone active in the Church	99%

Then we specifically invited, "List other important goals that you have as a family." That list included:

Being good Christians and good citizens	37%
Putting the family first	22%
Business success	16%

Work	10%
Grades	2%
Health	2%
Sports	1%

It comes as no surprise that the parents wanted their children to be active in the Church, go on missions, and marry in the temple. We have discussed their support of public education in chapter 5 and how they developed family unity in chapter 3. This chapter will concentrate on feelings the parents expressed about developing self-esteem in their children and on the individual goals that each couple articulated for their own family.

DEVELOPING SELF-ESTEEM IN CHILDREN

A wide range of studies have shown the importance of children's feelings of self worth as an influence in their decisions and actions. Those who have a poor self concept are more likely to engage in self-defeating behaviors. It is also clear from the research in this area that children's self concept is learned, particularly as they hear others talk about them or compare them to others in either positive or negative terms. Since these comparisons are most often made with other family members, friends, or relatives, the influence of these people on children's self worth is vital.

On the chart where we asked for demographic data (like age and sex) for each individual in the family, we also asked parents to evaluate "each person's feelings of self-worth: 1-High, 2-Medium, 3-Low." We assumed that there would be an implied comparison with others that they knew. Here are the ratings:

	Husbands' Self-Esteem	*Wives' Self-Esteem*
High	73%	64%
Medium	23%	33%
Low	3%	2%

In reporting results for the children, parents rated 75 percent of them with high feelings of self-worth, 20-25 percent with medium, and only 1-2 percent with low. The only real variation from this pattern was that the third child generally rated lower: 53 percent high and 46 percent as medium. (There is nothing in birth-order research that might provide a reason for this.)

None of this is a surprise. Positive people come out of a positive environment and, in turn, reinforce positive feelings for each other. When couples added comments on self-esteem, it was usually to describe a problem. One couple explained that one of their children had had low self-esteem from babyhood, and that being consistently positive and nurturing had been a great challenge for them. Another couple, in which the wife rated her feelings of self-worth as low and the husband as medium, had four children, all of them either medium or low as well. "We tried," they commented briefly opposite the line about helping each child develop self-worth.

A Utah mother with seven children listed as an adversity "one child with low self-esteem from birth" and commented, "It was long and slow to work out but has been done, I'm grateful to say. We handled it with much talk and love and patience and talk and patience and love and then still more."

A Utah mother rated her seven children and herself high in self-esteem (the husband's rating was blank), and explained that one of the important factors in making their family strong was "building high self-esteem through a positive, nurturing, loving attitude toward the children, encouraging them to choose the right and showing them what right is, and manifesting a commitment to the marriage, the family, and the Church." A California mother with three sons, jotted down by the question on self-worth: "If we can accomplish this one, then all the others will be easier."

An Idaho couple with three children rated everyone in the family as having medium self-worth. The mother noted, next to the goal of helping each child develop self-worth, "This is the hardest to do." One Salt Lake City mother with ten adopted children described their greatest challenge as a couple: "Helping the children have a good self image and not always succeeding." Then she articulated their family philosophy: "We know that we are here to help one another. Knowing that we are an eternal family also tells us that we must work out our problems and difficulties. We keep telling our children that we are experiencing the *adventure* of our lives—this life on earth—and to accept it as such. When you're down, don't stay down, because there's always something around the corner. And most importantly, we teach our children that everyone is here to learn and that some have progressed more than others. Everyone must be accepted for the level they are on, but do not allow whatever level they are on to affect you and how you act. Love God and serve and keep your testimony in spite of bad experiences. Have a good sense of humor. Go for it!"

WHAT EFFECTIVE FAMILIES WANT

About 25 percent of the couples did not add any additional goals to the checklist we provided, but they made some of the most interesting reading in the entire questionnaire, and we followed up in some of the interviews on topics brought up there. Many of the goals were related to topics already discussed, such as maintaining warm affection and strong unity. Some typical comments were "Taking care of each other in need"; "Maintaining strong family ties after the children leave home"; "Staying close as a family and as an extended family"; "Continuing the close-knit family unity in generations to come, with my husband and me still at the head of our extended family, worthy and qualified to give counsel and advice"; "Rendering assistance to the children's grandparents and other older people"; "Having the family love and enjoy one another"; "Doing things together and including the extended family"; and "Participating in activities together." Several couples mentioned attendance at family reunions as a goal, and one couple with four children, two of them married, described a "family cruise" as a goal.

Gospel-related Goals

Many couples said things like "Be a celestial family," "Attain the celestial kingdom," "Eternal life," and "Be together eternally." A Utah couple with nine children, all five of the married children with temple marriages and all of the sons who were old enough having served missions, wrote, "Our biggest goal is to learn to listen and understand and *follow* the promptings that come to us from the Holy Ghost." This was the same couple who had consciously taught their children to pray and listen for the guidance of the Holy Ghost from babyhood and who, when the children needed discipline, asked them to pray and listen to the Spirit.

A Texas couple in their fifties with four daughters, the youngest one twenty and a stake missionary, have the goal of going on missions themselves. A Utah couple have as a goal, "Internalizing the principles of the gospel." A California couple lists as a family goal, "To be strong Christians and serve the Lord all our lives." An Idaho couple with six daughters "would like each of our girls to be happily married and have a good family; and we'd like all of us to be together in the celestial kingdom." Two of their daughters are married, one with one child and the other with four, and a third daughter is divorced. An Idaho couple with five living children, only the oldest married, wanted their children to "marry and raise a good strong family and be better people than their parents." The Idaho farmer with twenty-one children by four marriages lists as goals for his children: "Always support Church authorities, always have and use a temple recommend, and maintain individual integrity" along with "being financially independent." An Idaho couple with seven children wanted, "happiness for each member." One Salt Lake City couple with five children, four of them married and with eight grandchildren among them, reflected their own delight in family life by listing as a goal, "Seeing the children with families of their own." A Wyoming couple with three children, none of them married yet, hopes for "happy marriages" as a major goal.

One Wyoming couple had had two sons killed at ages nine and seven. For them, an important goal was "to be a celestial family and be with the two that have gone on ahead of us." A Utah couple with seven children, six living, put "enduring to the end" as a family goal. A Salt Lake City couple with two sons and three daughters wrote they wanted their children to "keep a proper perspective on what is really worthwhile in life—who you are and not how much you have."

Educational and Economic Goals

Financial stability and security appeared as a goal on a significant number of couples' lists. A Salt Lake City couple with six children, all of them college graduates except for a son who is a college junior, wrote that a family goal was to "help each one get started in their own homes, businesses, and so on." A Texas couple with five temple-married daughters and one son waiting for his mission call had wanted to have their children "be self-reliant and dependable." A Provo professor and his wife with six children, three sons and three daughters, listed as an important goal, "Becoming good providers and being financially sound." For one Idaho family of seven, the goal was to "have each child able to function as a mature, responsible, independent person as early as possible."

A Montana farm couple want their eight children to "have a good business and be able to live comfortably." An Idaho couple (the husband is a travel agent and the wife is a teacher) want their four children, ages twenty-six to eighteen, to "succeed in their professions." The California parents of seven children say that "to be ambitious" is one of their family rules. A Utah couple with eight children at regular two-year intervals, none of them married and two on

144

missions (the eldest daughter also served a mission), list "financial management" and "helping others."

Other parents said, "Have each person prepared for an occupation"; "Make the farm pay"; "Live within our means"; "Be financially secure"; "Have a satisfactory profession that suits their abilities and interests"; "Learn the importance of work"; "Achieve economic independence"; "Have independence from parents"; "Be out of debt"; "Learn the work ethic"; and "Have strong career goals."

Some of these professional goals are broad enough to include more general self-development and educational goals. A Provo couple with seven children in which the father and the oldest son are both college professors list as goals, "Discovering and developing talents. Developing a love for truth and learning." An Idaho farm family with seven children want each "to develop their talents and interests." A Utah couple with seven children say they "expect each to find his or her special talent or interest and excell in it. Finances are not a high goal, nor is competitiveness." All of these children are making above-average grades in school; one is in medical school and another is a music student at the college level. One Wyoming couple with seven children said that an important goal for their family was, "Don't interfere with private time. Let each child choose to enjoy his or her special interests." A Salt Lake City couple with five daughters and a son has set the goal of developing musical and athletic talents. For a Wyoming family with seven living children, four daughters and three sons, Eagle Scout awards for the boys and the honor roll for everyone were high priorities. For one Provo family, a strong goal was "to acquire culture and an appreciation of the arts."

Relationship Goals

Many couples mentioned the importance of communication and related skills as family goals. In addition, others listed the kinds of qualities that would foster good relationships for their children. An Idaho family with ten children works hard "to teach the children manners and behavior that will help them be welcomed wherever they may go. We especially teach them to be appreciative of the things others do for them (especially their Father in heaven for his blessings) and to express thanks easily." An Idaho couple with three children lists as a family goal, "Be sensitive to and care for other people." A Utah couple with nine children has as a goal, "Improving love at home." A Utah couple with two sons and three daughters, all married except for one daughter who is engaged, wrote that a goal was "keeping lines of communication open among family members and in our own individual families."

For a Utah couple with eight unmarried children ranging in age from two to twenty-one, "respect for others" is a family goal. An Idaho couple with seven children listed "having a sense of humor." A Utah mother of three listed, "Have fun as a family." An Idaho couple with seven children listed "cheerfulness" as a family priority. A Montana blended family valued "honesty and communication." Another family wanted their children to "learn to reverence all of God's creations, recognize the right of all to their opinions, and learn the absolute necessity of being kind."

Service Goals

Many couples listed "service," "being good citizens," "patriotism" "loyalty to country with a knowledge of correct economic and political principles upon which the nation was founded," or being "responsible members of the community" among their family goals or as the most important family goal added to the checklist. A Utah couple with eight sons and a daughter have seen all of the boys but the sixteen-year-old serve missions and the six marriages performed in the temple. One of their important family goals was to "be useful citizens and neighbors, helping others with their means, time, and talents." A Utah couple with seven children said: "We want our children to be responsible workers and serve the community. We think it is important to plant more than we harvest, to help others less fortunate." One Texas couple (the father is a physician and the mother is an artist) wrote as a family goal: "Be an asset to the community."

CONCLUSION

Plans are not always accomplished as parents would like. Many of the parents pointed out that despite their best efforts, sometimes a child, or maybe two, had drifted away from the pattern or plan of the family. Parents were aware that they had made mistakes in implementing their plans. Sometimes they felt they were too strict, or maybe not strict enough. At times they might have given too much to one child and not enough to another. The children made mistakes, and the parents did not always know just how to respond. One Montana mother probably spoke for many parents when she looked at five mission-age sons, only one of whom had filled a mission, and confessed, "Some hopes went down the tubes."

But despite certain weaknesses and some failures, these parents had a vision of where they wanted to go and some understanding as to what they needed to do to get there. Many of the families seemed to evaluate their progress continually. This began with the couple talking together to assess how they were doing as parents and how well their children seemed to be doing. As they sensed the need for new directions and shifts in some areas, they might have held a family discussion, perhaps a family home evening, where the family planned to correct their course. At times this correction may have involved the entire family; at other times, it might have been directed toward one person who was not measuring up.

Successful parents seemed to know the state of the family. They saw their goals and their progress and sort of tapped things back into shape periodically. The knowledge of where they were and what was needed required husbands and wives who understood one another and wanted to get the job done. In contrast, one of the less-effective mothers confessed, "I don't know, but we're just at the stage where we have several teenagers, and they're acting just about like we did when we were younger. We've attempted to fix the problems up, but it never works as well as we hope it will. I guess we'll just live with it and maybe the kids will shape up when they get married. That's our only hope, I guess." In sharp contrast—not with satisfaction but with commitment—stands the comment of one Salt Lake City mother of eight children, seven of them living. She wrote that one of their most important family goals was "to have joy," then added a candid progress report: "I think we will not know if we have raised a successful family until we see how our grandkids turn out. Also I must admit I think we would not have had as much success as we have had if we had insisted on following every Church plan to perfection. We cannot really separate our family and the Church, but in some instances, our family has had first priority when it came to choosing how we would spend our time, yet our children all know the Church is first in our lives—without them having to be scond. We are not a perfect family. We have a long way to go, but we are all on the way. For this we are grateful, yet humbled by our shortcomings. We want to be better. We will be! Twenty years from now, if we are identified as a successful family, it will be more believable. Right now, we think it is premature."

Chapter Twelve

HOW TO CHANGE
YOUR FAMILY

It seems logical that many Latter-day Saints who read this book might ask, "How may we become a more effective family?" You may have preschoolers and elementary-school-age children, perhaps with new babies still coming. Or perhaps your children are teenagers or even adults living at home. The good news (we suppose it could also be the bad news) is that there is no particular age or stage when parenting is automatically easier. We asked the parents in our survey four questions:

1. At what age have you found your children the easiest to rear?
2. Why do you think that is?
3. At what age have you found your children the most difficult to rear?
4. Why do you think that is?

Sixteen percent of the parents responded that they had found all times equally easy, and 2 percent said they had never found an easy time. But the remainder of those who responded made a pattern that looked like this:

Age	Easiest to Rear	Hardest to Rear
0- 5	26%	8%
6-12	37%	5%
13-15	9%	41%
16-18	3%	32%
19-21	3%	4%
over 21	2%	1%

It will be a surprise to no one that 73 percent of the families identified the teen years as the hardest, although it was interesting that the earlier teen years seemed to involve more difficulties than the later teens. Even so, 12 percent of the parents found the teenage years the easiest of any stage.

When we asked the parents to give the reasons for their answers, the pattern, again not suprisingly, revolved around authority and individualism, again showing that Mormon families are not much different from American families in general. Twenty-six percent of the parents said that preschoolers were easiest to rear with an additional 37 percent opting for the six-to-twelve age group. Of these parents, 40 percent cited the willingness of their children to accept guidance as the reason, while 22 percent gave as a reason that it was easier to talk things over and the child was more likely to accept the parent's reasoning. Fifty-nine percent of the parents who said the teenage years were the hardest cited the child's increasing need for autonomy as the reason. Twenty-three percent cited peer influence and outside activities as the reason these years were so difficult.

Many parents added comments on the questionnaire or during interviews about why they responded as they did. A Provo couple with eight children, ages seven to twenty-three, said that "all ages" were easy to rear because of their particular family structure: "The wife worked most with the children when they were younger, and the husband when they were older." They had two sons, a daughter, another son, and then four daughters, and they had checked that while both parents were equally responsible for teaching, helping, and disciplining the children between the ages of six and twelve, that the husband took over decisions about the duties and behavior of the boys after age six while the wife continued to make most of the decisions about the duties and behavior of the girls.

A mother whose two children were born a year apart when her husband's four children by his first marriage were between nineteen and twelve acknowledged that "nothing but love and patience can build trust and unity in a step-parent situation" but exclaimed, "I find children absolutely fascinating and fun at each stage of development." The Idaho parents of ten children ranging in age from twelve to twenty-nine corroborated, "Every age has its special problems and its very special joys. Each child had a difficult period or so, but on the whole, we have thoroughly enjoyed every age of every child."

An Idaho mother of six children, ages sixteen to thirty-four, wrote, "Every year I wished that time would stand still. Raising children was such a wonderful joy and challenge. If I had to choose, I'd say the early teens were the hardest. The children had to become adults, and parents had to make the transition from rule givers to friends. It's a time for learning for all of us."

A Salt Lake City couple with three sons and three daughters, all of them married except for one daughter who was just completing a mission, observed, "There's no easy time. It's always a challenge," but added, "We enjoyed all ages. It's just that each age has different difficulties."

One couple from Idaho with two daughters and two sons between ages twenty-nine and twenty-two, all married, had very precise memories about hard and easy ages. "Six was easiest," they recalled, "because the world was more frightening to them and they were more willing to listen and seek parental help. Fifteen was hardest because of their wanting to be independent and because of peer pressure."

Some parents saw the preschool years as easiest. The California parents of three living children wrote that the first year of life was easiest: "They were cuddly, cute, and cooperative."

Another mother, who also found that the preschool years were easiest, wrote: "In many respects, there was more work to be done when all of the children were little and we had two or three in diapers at the same time. But every day there was a quiet time when all of the children were in bed—bathed and looking so clean and sweetly asleep. We always knew pretty much where they were; and while there were quarrels and tiffs, we usually could settle things.

"Now that most of the children are teenagers, it's a different world. They want to be gone all the time, and we have to keep insisting that they tell us where they are going and when they will be back. They want to go places, do things, and wear things we don't feel too good about, but they say, 'Everyone else does it. Why can't we?'

"We know they get hurt or upset, but it isn't easy anymore to talk with them about their problems. When they were little, they brought every little problem or concern to us, but that has really changed. Dad and I often feel like strangers on the outside wanting to help but not knowing how to get in.

"We recall how we used to say we would be so thankful when we got all the kids out of diapers, into school, and had some time to ourselves. But now I can see that those early years were really less complicated and worrisome than things are now."

Several couples liked the age from babyhood to two because it was less trouble then the other ages, but that seemed to be largely a matter of spacing. One Provo couple with three children born in three years and a fourth coming four years later recalls those first three years as the most difficult "because we were most restricted. The father had less time because of being in school. We had less money. We got less sleep. The children demanded constant attention, and we had less freedom."

A Utah couple with nine children, ages eight, to twenty-seven, liked ages six to twelve because "they can care for themselves but they're still teachable and there isn't as much peer pressure. After fourteen, they found their children "testing rules, striving for independence, subject to peer pressure, and involved in proving themselves to their peers and to themselves." A Utah couple with fourteen children, ages seven to thirty, also thought of the years between six and twelve as easy: "They are beyond usual childhood diseases, and they haven't yet thought of dating, driving cars, and so on." A Provo couple with seven living children, ages twelve to twenty-nine, exuberantly wrote for easiest age: "Six to twelve and twenty-plus! No diapers and no teenagers!"

One Utah father with five sons, ages twenty-two to thirty and with two of them now married, observed: "The golden years in our family were the teenage period. Our fourth child was born when the first was turning five, and our fifth arrived three years later. My recollection of those early years is one of lots of work, sick kids, and heavy physical demands. For about five of those years, I was a bishop or had heavy Church responsibilities, and my wife had a great deal of work and responsibility.

"However, when the boys were all teenagers, they could either drive or go with someone besides the parents. Everything seemed to happen at our house—parties, song practices, play rehearsals, and student-body-election committee meetings. Loud music was always competing with somebody on the guitar or piano. The food bill was astronomical. We spent all of our time going to ball games, plays, and programs. I loved it.

"And there were never any real problems with our children. There were the usual romances and breakups, lost elections and football games, a constant hassle about neglected chores; but we did a lot of things together—skiing, fishing, golfing, ball games, and great family trips and vacations. We liked being together, and the talk was always rich and stimulating. Underneath it all was the knowledge that in just a few years our boys would all be on missions. We savored the crowded years that were passing so rapidly. At least in my mind, these years were the easiest."

CONDITIONS NECESSARY FOR CHANGE

Even if change is desirable, is it possible? One Montana couple had been raised in inactive homes and did not become active themselves until the first four of their seven children were already in their teens. They saw the absence of Church influence in those early years as crucial. One son had run away several times. A second preferred non-Mormon friends. One son had served a mission and married in the temple, but his brother and the two daughters had not. The contrast with the younger children, they felt, was marked. But does that mean change is impossible if a family starts out in a direction it later wants to alter?

Not necessarily. A great deal of research has been done on how and why people change. Two conditions seem to be absolutely essential for change to occur:

1. People change only when they *feel a strong need to change*. The research has looked at religious conversion, management training, Weight-Watchers, and Alcoholics Anonymous. Unless people "sign up" feeling powerfully, even desperately, that they need to change, just sitting through the program and going through the motions won't do it. Before a family can change, at least one person in that family has to say, "We cannot let our family continue to go on as it has. Things aren't right. I'm going to do absolutely everything in my power to help make things better."

2. People change when someone they respect agrees with them and supports the change. Alcoholics Anonymous assigns each person a "buddy" who has overcome the problem and who will be on call for as long as the person needs help. If the wife is the one who feels that something has to change, the husband too needs to support the change. Then if the couple has a friend, a parent, a bishop, or home teachers who can give support, encouragement, or suggestions, the chances for success increase further.

Newly converted parents often pray for the first time with a missionary acting as the model for prayer and also as an authority figure in asking for the prayer to be said. Both parents and children accept holding family prayer because they accept the new teaching situation. In other words, this family has both social support and someone to initiate the change in learning to pray. In the family setting, the parents must usually initiate the change; but usually they can do it simply by announcing that they are going to change something or, better still, holding a family discussion about what needs to change and how.

The "how" is important. It is not enough for a couple to say, "We need to start talking together more." A more effective plan would be: "We are going to do three things: (1) Every night (or twice a week) before the children go to bed, we will all meet in the parents' bedroom, talk about the day's events or things coming up, or share some memories of times past, and then have family prayer together. (2) We parents will make a list of gospel topics and questions. During Sunday dinner, you children can choose one of these topics for discussion, or you may take a turn telling the rest of us what you learned in church that day. We'll say what we learned, too. (3) On Fast Sunday (or another specified time during the month), the father will have a personal interview with each child. In the interview they will talk about any concerns the child has, any issues the parents want to raise, and goals that the child wants to set."

If the program were this clear, if everyone in the family agreed on it, and if the parents were willing to pour the energy it takes into seeing that it actually happens, every day, every week, every month, then change would come.

A real roadblock to change is how much effort it takes. People simply get tired of putting all the necessary effort into a project until the new pattern feels comfortable. Also, most people are afraid of failing or looking inept when they try something new. One father ruefully reported what happened when he tried making a change: "I was not satisified with the degree of closeness we had in our family. We didn't talk together or do much together. We all seemed to be going in different directions. I was determined to bring the family closer and had an image of our family enjoying lively discussions together. So I told my wife and our three children (ages nine, twelve, and fourteen) that I wanted everyone to be at dinner promptly that evening. We were all going to sit around and have a good time talking. When they weren't at the table on time, I yelled at everyone and finally got them seated. Then I asked my son, 'What did you do today at school?' 'Nothing.' 'Anything ineresting happen?' 'Nope.' I got the same non-response from the rest of the kids. The phone rang and they all jumped up to get it, and I decided to forget the whole thing."

Similarly, if a family has never held a family home evening before, the parents may feel very anxious about trying this new activity. And since the children will be resisting change for exactly the same reason, the anxiety has some justification in fact. One father in an active family that conscientiously tried to have a regular family home evening revealed some of the problems: "There's an old saying in the Church that family home evening is the only fight that is opened and closed with prayer. That isn't exactly how our family night sessions are, but they aren't as effective as my wife and I would like. First, one or more of the kids is often busy and either doesn't want to have family night or wants to cut it short. Then the age differences among the children sometimes make it difficult to get everyone interested in a topic. I think our best lessons have been those where the children give the lesson to the rest of the family."

The next problem is how to get the children behind the change, not just putting up with it to accommodate Mom and Dad. In addition to just plain sticking with it until the dinner-table conversation becomes expected and a habit, how can you encourage the children to invest in it and see that they too are benefiting?

One way is to keep the goal clear. Say, "I really enjoy dinnertime now. I enjoy learning what you kids thought

156

about Brother Miller's talk. I feel that we're learning to communicate better as a family." Or make the topic of conversation clear enough that the "rules" for participation are clear: "Jane told me something vey interesting about alternative energy forms that they discussed in school today. Why don't you tell them about it, Jane? Do you have any ideas, Stan, on which forms might be most practical in this area?"

Another suggestion is to reward people for their participation: "I really appreciate Bart's suggestion that we broaden the topics to include current events. I though at first that we needed to concentrate on gospel topics; but they have a way of creeping into everything anyway."

Deal with resistance and negative behavior in terms of the goal, not the person: "Rob, we've all decided that we want to improve how our family communicates. When you call Susan a nerd because she likes the president, does that help our family or hurt it? What will you do to help?"

Let the children articulate their feelings about what's happening as they work toward the goal: "Susan, you and Rob had quite a debate about the president tonight, and in the past, that's been quite a sore point between you sometimes. How did you feel about tonight's discussion?"

CASE STUDIES

In light of these suggestions, let us share with you two case studies of Latter-day Saint families we interviewed that made a decided change. We've altered the names and certain other information to safeguard their privacy.

Jack grew up in a community just outside of Salt Lake City in a solid working-class family—the father was a crane operator—that was known as a good Latter-day Saint family, even though the father worked most Sundays and could only attend church irregularly. Jack was active while he was growing up, but when he enlisted in the navy at seventeen for World War II, he was never stationed near a branch. Naturally, he could not attend church. None of his new companions were Latter-day Saints, and he went along with them, drinking coffee and occasionally drinking with them on shore leave.

Discharged at age twenty, Jack went back home and found that most of his high-school friends were also inactive. He didn't go back to church. After several months, he met Betty, and they began dating seriously. She was an active Church member from an active family, but she fell in love. To her parents' disappointment, she married Jack outside the temple.

They moved to another community in the Salt Lake City area. Jack was ambitious and hard working. He took a weekend job and also started to build their house on weekends. For more than eight years, Betty went to meetings periodically, but Jack was a virtual stranger in the ward.

They had four sons; and as the boys got old enough to attend Primary and Sunday School, Jack and Betty began to have a series of talks together about their future as a family, largely initiated by Betty. They discussed at length what they wanted for their sons. For both, it included active Church membership.

During their entire marriage, Jack and Betty knew that Jack's mother and Betty's parents hoped they would return to activity in the Church. They never criticized or pressured Jack and Betty, but Jack always knew that they would be deeply pleased if he became active again. And he knew it was mostly up to him, since Betty was already quite committed to activity.

While Jack and Betty were having these discussions, the elders quorum president in their ward began to visit them, encouraging Jack to attend priesthood meetings with him. Betty and Jack both respected him and considered him a friend, so Jack somewhat reluctantly accepted the invitation and began to attend more regularly. As his confidence grew, he was asked to teach a Sunday School class and accepted.

Then Jack was offered an attractive job in another part of the state, and they moved to a new location. They might have drifted back into inactivity, but their new bishop noticed that they had two boys who were Cub Scout age and called Betty to be a den mother and Jack a cubmaster. Soon they were thoroughly involved in the ward. They agreed to attend a Project Temple series, again at the bishop's invitation, and were sealed in the temple. Other ward positions came for both of them. Jack was called as a counselor in the bishopric, then as bishop. After a long time in this key position, he was made a member of the stake high council. Betty served in several auxiliary positions and then in the stake Relief Society presidency. Three of their four boys filled missions and all married in the temple. Jack and Betty had turned their lives around and made a permanent difference in the lives of their children.

All of the elements were present to encourage and support change. Jack and Betty felt a deep need to make a change. The elders quorum president gave a Jack a specific invitation to do something in his company and with his approval by attending meetings. He was present to ease the shock of going back, and he supported Jack emotionally. Jack's mother and Betty's parents were openly delighted and very supportive. The children had already been attending Primary and Sunday School, so the change was not drastic for them. Besides, since they were young, they were very willing to go along with the decision of their parents. As Jack and Betty became more active, they were rewarded by feeling more integrated into the ward, developed a wider circle of friends, and accepted positions that gave them more support, more status, and more positive reinforcement. At some point, they were fully active, not for the sake of their sons, but because they themselves were benefiting from it and fully believed in it. Going to the temple not only rewarded them with the knowledge that their family was now sealed forever, if they would continue worthy, but also articulated new covenants of devotion to the gospel.

The youthful ages of their sons was certainly an advantage for Jack and Betty in making the change. In the second case study, Scott and Paula needed to make the change operate effectively for their teenage children as well. Scott came from a very strong Latter-day Saint family and was a returned missionary. Paula's family were inactive members, and Paula had never been active. She attended Brigham Young University because it was convenient, and there they met, fell in love, and married. Then they moved to California. They also had four sons.

Scott attended church fairly regularly and held a few positions, while Paula was almost completely inactive, smoked, drank coffee, and had an occasional cocktail. Their boys were baptized at eight and attended church with Scott.

Then one Sunday when their oldest boy was about sixteen and the youngest was nine, the stake president phoned, asking Scott to come to his office and bring Paula. With some foreboding, Scott agreed. The stake president told them that their ward was being divided. The new bishop wanted Scott to be one of his counselors. Would Scott accept the call and would Paula support him? Scott said, "President, I am honored to receive this call, but my wife and I are not worthy." The stake president looked at both of them and said, "You can get worthy, can't you?" Scott and Paula looked at each other and, with that ability married couples gain through the years, communicated with each other and agreed. Scott replied, "Yes, President, we can and will get worthy, and we accept the call."

In a daze they went home, called their sons around them, and told them of the new call. The boys were delighted and enthusiastic. They talked for some time about the changes all of them would have to make to be worthy of this new calling. Paula pledged never to use coffee, tea, alcohol, or tobacco again. They all agreed to start having prayer, going to church together, paying a full tithing, and having family home evening.

Making the decision was the easy part. Scott, the most religiously trained partner in the marriage, was gone a great deal with his new calling, leaving Paula, who was less experienced, to carry out many of the decisions. Sometimes they forgot. Sometimes they weren't prepared. Both Scott and Paula were determined to make the changes, however, and after several weeks the new activities became routine and began to feel "normal." Within a year Paula was called to serve in the ward Primary presidency. Their eldest son turned mission age and accepted a mission call. His three brothers followed in his footsteps. The family became one of the stake stalwarts. Paula found she enjoyed the temple and attended frequently. Later she became stake Relief Society president, and Scott served on the high council. This family was truly transformed.

For Scott and Paula, the need to change was stimulated by an important new Church calling. Both the bishop and the stake president were important people giving support and encouragement. All of the boys rallied around and provided the needed family social support. It made the change work.

These two case studies happen to be success stories. There is no guarantee that older children will support a change, even when the parents are totally behind it; but it is certain that weak commitment and uncertainty on the part of the parents will doom change before it begins.

One father talked about his reluctance to start a needed change. He said, "We have never had family prayer in our home. I feel it would be a great strength to all of us if we started this practice. But I don't know how to begin. I'm afraid that if I try it, my kids will all snicker and make fun of the whole idea. After all, they have never even heard me pray aloud, and I don't know how anyone would react." His fears are not unrealistic, but it is doubtful if he will be able to get anything started, feeling the way he does.

A possible approach might be: "Children, when I grew up we used to have family prayer in our home. This we did every morning and evening. The same thing happened in your mother's home. For some reason we just didn't get prayer started in our home. Mother and I have talked about it, and we want to begin to have family prayers together in

161

our home. We would like to do this just before we eat breakfast and before dinner at night. We hope that all of you will come and kneel with us so we can have prayer together. This will help us as a family. We love each of you and want to do what is right."

CONCLUSION

If nothing else, the record of the highly effective families in this study should encourage parents about the possibility of changing. The parents of nine children, ranging in age from thirteen to twenty-nine, wrote: "We are trying with all our hearts to be an eternal family, and we do this unitedly. Even though we do not succeed always, we are trying. Inch by inch, day by day, line upon line, we shall continue to strive for that greatest of all goals—being an eternal family and having exaltation."

Chapter Thirteen

FACING THE FUTURE

Since doing this research, we've talked with many young Mormon couples who are engaged, newly wed, or parents of a new baby. They ask us if our research applies to them. The world they face seems very different from that of our 200 families, whose children are either launched on their own or are within a few years of leaving.

We think the answer is yes; but they will also have to consider that they are different from our survey families in many ways. What are some of these differences?

The percentage of converts in the Church is steadily growing larger. Will these numbers tip the Mormon tradition toward more "worldly" values when it comes to raising strong, Church-centered families? In our opinion, this should not be a major challenge. Mormons did not invent strong families. Almost every religious tradition enhances and encourages family life. And despite the bad press on families, the institution of the family is still—and probably always will be—a prime American value as well.

For instance, researchers Nick Stinnett and John Defrain describe *Secrets of Strong Families* (New York: Little, Brown, 1985) based on a sample of 3,000 families from a variety of religious backgrounds. Here are some of the characteristics they found that strong families have in common:

1. Commitment. They put the family first in their lives and see it as the strongest influence on them.

2. Communication. They talk about issues when they

come up. They don't run away from problems or sit on them.

3. Time. They spend quality time together—and do it in great quantities.

4. Spiritual wellness. They have strong spiritual values and are concerned with other people.

5. Coping with crises. All families faced some crises but coped with them as an opportunity for change and growth.

Do these findings sound familiar? What they tell us, as family researchers, is that families are healthy across the nation. The Church doesn't have all the good families. Alarm about the "disappearing" American family, or about the family slipping into a slough of greedy materialism, seems decidedly misplaced. Furthermore, building better families will probably get more emphasis nationally in the years ahead. Converts who came from strong families will find only support for values they already espouse.

"Strong" does not, however, necessarily mean "traditional." Currently fewer than 25 percent of American families fit the pattern of a full-time homemaker/mother and full-time wage-earning father. In the younger families especially, both couples are likely to be employed and also share child-care and homemaking responsibilities, although this division of labor is far from equally shared in most cases, and the woman is usually most heavily burdened. In such cases, couples must usually make a decision to have fewer children or else to have at least one parent at a time limit his or her career development to spend more time with the children. Although the research is far from final on dual-career couples, parents who have the energy, resources, and commitment *are* able to provide high-quality parenting and maintain satisfying careers simultaneously. Probably more and more young couples will move into this pattern, although some who are not suited for it by personality are forced into it by economic necessity.

By far the greatest increase, however, has come among

single-parent families. Approximately 11 million American children—20 percent of the nation's youngsters—are currently being raised by their mother alone. Another 1 million are being raised by their father alone. Sixty percent of black children and 33 percent of white children have divorced parents.

Latter-day Saints who marry in the temple have a divorce rate of 6 percent, while 30 percent of Mormons married out of the temple have been divorced. Nationally, 23 percent of "ever married" people have been divorced. About 65 percent of all Latter-day Saints households have a married couple in them, while about 35 percent are single-adult households. About 4 percent of Latter-day Saint households consist of children and a single parent.

All of this means a shift in the traditional pattern of the family. Parents will be under much greater pressure to plan well the time they have available for their children, particularly if they are parenting without partners. As this study shows, mothers have spent more time with the children than the fathers have—talking with them, checking on direction and problems, monitoring situations, and acting as an early warning system to bring the father's attention to bear on problems that the mother spots. In the future, both parents, not just the mother, will need to spend quality time with the children and to make family activities their highest priority. Even though work may still take the biggest chunk of time, we feel that the most creative and energetic thought should be spent on family life.

If two working parents (or a single parent) come home exhausted to children who have been doing nothing but watching television after school and sink down in front of their own favorite programs, the patterns that build effective families could be in jeopardy. Parents who are too tired to attend church, or too pinched financially to pay tithing, or too busy to have family prayer will not be able to teach these values to their own children.

Our data show that most LDS parents exercise some control over their children's television (either directly or by teaching them what constitutes appropriate viewing) and make schoolwork a high priority. Will busy parents allow children to watch more television as a way of freeing up time for themselves? If so, what will the results be if "media values" become the most dominant in the home?

Another real problem is complacency. Bill is president of a Brigham Young University stake. Over the past five years, attendance at sacrament meeting has remained constant; but attendance at priesthood meeting, Sunday School, and Relief Society has declined steadily along with home teaching and visiting teaching. When we talk to students about these trends, some frankly describe lessons from Church manuals as boring and some Church programs as irrelevant; but by far more serious and more frequent is the "it doesn't matter" feeling. "There's no real reason for me to feel that being active is essential," observed one. "The Church is so strong here that what I do or don't do doesn't make a difference to it." Others added, "Besides, everyone misses some meetings or goes to an R-rated movie. It's no big deal."

While we might agree about the quality of certain lessons or the lack of earthshaking consequences for going to an occasional R-rated movie, what we do see—very clearly—is that relativity is a slippery slide. Young people who don't have clear boundaries on their behavior and who keep waffling about what is or isn't important can be backed over the edge into serious transgression in a remarkably brief period of time. Furthermore, even if there are no dire immediate consequences, will these people, as parents, have firm convictions about what's right and wrong and the will to pass on these values to their children?

Another difference for the future is family size. The couples in our study averaged six children apiece. The average number of children ever born to Latter-day Saint families is now 3.3 compared to just over 2 for the average American family. There seems to be some evidence that

Latter-day Saint families are following the national trend downward. What differences might this trend make?

We can make some hypotheses. Parents with six children obviously cannot do all the work themselves. No matter how hard it is to get children to do chores, the children have to help. Also, with six children to provide for, the family income is stretched thin. To have extra money, children have to take jobs outside the family or work for what they get within it. If parents have smaller families, will they still have the same motivation and need to teach their children the work ethic?

Although the difference between one and two incomes in some Mormon families already spells the difference between whether the children can go on missions and college, at the same time personal income is generally rising across the nation. (Utah is fourth in per capita income [1981] but higher in family income. The mean earnings for families where the husband worked and the wife did not was $22,580 in the United States and $21,822 in Utah in 1979. When the wife also works full time, the mean is $27,644 [U.S.] and $25,855 [Utah]. Utah comes out lower on the per-capita income scale because of comparatively large numbers of people per household. [Jerry Mason, "Family Economics." Unpublished manuscript.]) The income distribution for Latter-day Saint families is not much different from national levels.

Mormon families are already, according to our data, concerned about keeping a nice home, going on vacations, and doing things together. Right now, these factors reflect the parents' emphasis on achieving greater family unity. It is possible, however, that they could be seen as ends in themselves rather than as means to an end; if so, then family unity may be one of the casualties of a more materialistic life-style.

Does this mean that we, as sociologists, advise young couples to plan a traditional marriage? Not necessarily. Certainly, we feel that the traditional model is an option that young couples should have available if they wish to make that choice and can sustain its demands. And certainly, there is nothing "easy" about a traditional marriage, any more than there is about a nontraditional marriage. However, we are not advising young people to choose that model without looking at it carefully, weighing its pros and cons, and considering other options as well. For instance, the stereotype of the traditional marriage could be described with these adjectives: "poor but happy," "hardworking and close," "lots of children and loving."

We see no virtue in poverty for its own sake. We've seen too often how financial tensions can absorb nearly all the emotional energies of a couple until there is nothing left to enrich the relationship. There can also be some negative consequences in a scenario where the husband is so concerned about providing for his family that he has neither time nor energy left over for parenting, and where the wife, who is having a baby every two years, is increasingly isolated in caring for the children, largely alone. It is usually her own academic interests and training that get put on hold, sometimes permanently, for the sake of the family. We see a great potential for happy family life in a pattern that allows—even insists— that both parents get to develop both their nurturing sides and their achieving sides simultaneously.

However, making this pattern work effectively will require a degree of intelligence, awareness, and flexible planning as the family moves from stage to stage that simply was not required of previous generations. The traditional pattern has worked and worked well largely because the assignment of tasks made it possible to keep the bases covered. If these tasks and roles have to be renegotiated every three to six months because of inevitable shifts in the family situation or activities, *that* could seem like an enormous amount of work—too much to be worth it. Actually, the communication skills required, the awareness of the needs of individual family members, and the choosing— time after time after time—to put family values and Church service first over other demands cannot help but have the same good results as those we see in highly effective traditional families. And what a lesson for children! But it's definitely not a scenario that fits every family.

We have every reason to believe that families of the future might respond quite differently to some items on a questionnaire such as ours that asks questions about activities, money, education, and chores. But we suspect that the answers about family strengths, family values, and feelings for each other would be just about the same. The task of building a strong family is one that has to be undertaken by each couple, no matter how successful or unsuccessful their own families were.

Our scenario for the future sees diversity. The principles of family building as emphasized by our Church leaders and described in Church magazines and lessons are still the same, but the actual forms into which these principles are translated are changing. We see not just one image of a successful family but many. We see a pattern of increasing pluralism where the emphasis is not on roles but on skills—the same skills of communication, teaching gospel principles, and developing competence as a variety of tasks that successful families in this study have discovered.

Despite the ugly side of our society—violence, unchastity, and materialism—it supports some family values in a way that earlier American society did not. It stresses problem solving, not just problem enduring. It puts a high value on communication skills. It recognizes the real satisfactions of achievement. It emphasizes planning and taking charge of the future. These societal values can and will reinforce important gospel values for thoughtful, sensitive parents who are committed to each other and to their children.

As authors, we've done most of our parenting, but we're cheering for our children as they become parents in turn. In some ways, we envy them. The future is going to be an exciting time to build strong families, and we wish them—and you—joy in the process.

Index